READER BONUS!

Dear Reader,

As a thank you for your support, the Authors of *Choose Confidence* would like to offer you a special reader bonus.

Go here to tap into the free gifts from the authors valued at more than $10,000: www.ChooseConfidence.com.

READER BONUS!

CHOOSE CONFIDENCE

THE DECISION —— TO —— EMBRACE YOUR POWER

Curator Information:
Email: molly@thepreparedperformer.com
Website: www.ChooseConfidence.com

Publisher Information:
Email: lynda@actiontakerspublishing.com
Website: www.actiontakerspublishing.com

ISBN # (paperback) 978-1-956665-88-8
ISBN # (Kindle) 978-1-956665-58-1

Table of Contents

"Commitment is the glue that holds courage
and creativity together."
~Molly Mahoney

Introduction

Confidence is a choice. It's a hidden skill waiting to be unlocked.

Unlocking your ability to choose confidence is the driving force behind this book. After helping thousands of people show up more confidently, I know confidence is the key to possibility.

Now, I'm not saying it's always an easy switch to flip. But it can be!

Confidence takes courage, creativity, and commitment.

These elements form the foundation of a confident life, empowering you to face challenges, embrace your uniqueness, and persist through obstacles, big and small.

Growing up, I was a musical theater kid dreaming of performing on the world's biggest stages. After booking gigs on cruise ships and in Vegas, I moved to New York to hit the audition scene and my confidence wavered. Surrounded by exceptional talent, I often felt inadequate. It wasn't until I embraced my unique qualities and stood tall in my authenticity that I discovered the true power of confidence.

This transformation led to booking shows nationwide, an international Broadway tour, and even a movie with Dick Van Dyke. It also inspired me to start my own marketing business, helping business owners show up and "perform" online. We've generated millions in revenue, reached millions with our content, and helped thousands of clients to make a real impact.

You might be skeptical about the idea of choosing confidence. I get it. Self-doubt and fear can be powerful forces. But this book will show you practical ways to overcome these barriers and build your confidence muscle.

In these pages, you'll learn:

1. Techniques to identify and challenge self-limiting beliefs
2. Strategies for authentically showing up in life and business
3. Methods to build resilience in the face of setbacks
4. Exercises to practice and strengthen your confidence daily

As a fierce form of activism, years ago I made a choice to #stand4joy. When I wrote my first children's book, Finding My Awesome, I saw the power of helping kiddos to be more confident through written word.

This book is my invitation to allow readers of all ages to step out, step up, and let their light shine! This is about spreading confidence and giving that gift to as many people as possible. I believe confidence is a skill we all need to develop. You have the power already—you just need to decide to strengthen your confidence muscle.

Confidence empowers you to face challenges head-on, make bold decisions, and stand up for your beliefs. Without confidence, even the most talented humans can fall behind, held back by self-doubt and fear. Confidence isn't just about believing in yourself; it's about taking action, pushing through barriers, and inspiring others to do the same.

As you dive into this book, hold onto your hats and glasses!

We can't wait to see the ripple effect you create as you unlock the magic within these pages.

Molly Mahoney

CHAPTER 1

Inner Power Awakened: The Path to Unshakeable Confidence by Defeating Imposter Syndrome

Barbara Jenks

To everyone who contributes to and supports my continuing personal growth journey, especially Andrea, Barbara, Leslie, Jackson, Trevor and NLP guru, Michael Bernoff - thank you for your encouragement and love on my way to the congruent me. And thank you, Molly, for this opportunity to tell my story.

Can you believe it's estimated that 85% of people worldwide have low self-esteem (Guttman, Jennifer Psy.D., "The Relationship with Yourself: Notes on self-confidence and authenticity," Psychology Today, 6/27/2019), and there's many who say this is particularly true of women?

Wow! *That* many people suffer from the same malaise I did for so long – low self-esteem that's fueled by lack of confidence, second-guessing, analysis paralysis, perfectionism, imposter syndrome? How can that be possible?! Back then, everyone looked so much more accomplished than me … so together … living their best life …. It never occurred to me that so many others were also stricken by the negative mindsets resulting from low self-esteem.

How about you? Have you ever felt overwhelmed and stressed by daily responsibilities and self-doubt, requiring perfection in everything? How do you cope with that? If you're like me, it was escaping into a pint of Ben and Jerry's at the end of the day—or like me a long time ago, escaping into a glass (or three) of wine. Yes, I lived many years of my life that way—but not anymore. What I didn't know back then is that one day I'd learn about Neuro-Linguistic Programming (NLP) and use it to rewire my negative thoughts. With this specialized technique, I'd tame my chronic over-thinking and radically transform my life. If it worked for me, it can work for you, too.

My first step toward the deeply rooted confidence I enjoy today sprang from great personal failure—coming face to face with alcoholism. My drive to drink several glasses of wine every day eclipsed all. I "drank at" everyone and everything to cope with emotions I didn't know how to process. On the outside I looked like I had it all—a good job, good friends, never arrested for drunk driving or any other trouble—but I needed alcohol to feel normal. Little did I know then that it wasn't the *drinking* but the out-of-control, nonstop negative *thinking* that drove the drinking. My own thinking made me feel that I was not ok.

No doubt you know people who began life like me: The kid in grammar school who had few friends—one of the many who faded

2

into the background and who lived in the pain of not measuring up to the other kids, always feeling like I was less than them somehow and feeling uncomfortable in my own skin. Not really knowing what I was supposed to do or who I was supposed to be, I was shuttled along with the others.

In high school I achieved a level of popularity that made it seem like I was fitting in, yet the feeling of separateness and not belonging continued to pulse in the background. That newfound approval opened doors to many great parties, and I discovered that fully partaking in those events quieted the background beat of unworthiness. So, I partied through high school and college, and into my first professional positions, with increasing dependence on a substance outside of me to quell my inner voice and make me feel okay. When drinking, I felt great—but when the alcohol wore off, I was still faced with a "me" that I liked less and less, which fed a vicious cycle of uncomfortably harsh self-critical thoughts that required more and more drink to quiet down so I could get some relief. Ultimately, my alcoholism caught up with me—there wasn't enough drink in the world that would stop the self-loathing and make me feel comfortable in my own skin. I had my last drink in my late 20s, but my trek toward confidence was just beginning.

In early sobriety, I had acquired enough experience to ascend in an HR career, which constructed "exterior" confidence—the stuff the outer world can see, like career and other achievements. Although I felt authentic most of the time, my "self" was moored in the outer accomplishments. That exterior evidence did not translate to confident thoughts and feelings about me (interior confidence). To the contrary—my interior confidence was low—I did not trust myself, got lost in overthinking and analyzing, avoided risk, felt like I was hiding and not fully living up to my potential. I avoided putting myself out there—and when being front and center was required in my position (as it often was), I donned my "false self-suit," and put on a show. Now, if you asked me at the time, I would have told you, "This is who I am," that I was being authentic, and I looked confident to the audience. However, there was always a vague sense that I wasn't enough. I often fell into the negative spiral of self-doubt and judgmental self-talk, telling myself things like "you're an idiot," "you don't really know what you're doing," "you're not good enough" ... can you relate?

Yet, I kept getting promoted—a double-edged sword that ignited self-doubt and fear. To this day I can feel the tightness in my throat and the shallow breaths that accompanied self-doubt and fear. This is what imposter syndrome feels like—"that's not really me" and feeling like a fraud. As a single mom, it never occurred to me there was any other way. I had to make a living to support myself and my kids, so the onward and upward movement continued, constructing more layers of armor. At night, the coping mechanism of choice was Ben and Jerry's while sitting on the couch watching mindless TV.

This continued for many years until it all came to a screeching halt—I was laid off. Just like the back end of a car continues moving after the front end hits a wall, the facts of my life came barreling toward me very quickly after I hit the "you don't have a job" wall. Without the position and the title, I had little knowledge of who "I" was. I had poured myself so ardently into my profession that my entire identity became who I was in business. My work had morphed into an addiction, and just like the drinking, had kept my thoughts focused on external, not internal, evidence to anchor my self-esteem and confidence. The flurry of external activity fueling the one-woman show of juggling and balancing it all—kids, career, maintaining a home—was suddenly gone.

Like many career women who relegated child rearing to second position, I prioritized "the problem of the moment" at work. Once I found the way out of this thinking and learned how to pause, examine, change my thoughts and take different actions, I discovered I was driven by something my father told me when I was small: "Your work is your worth." And he meant hard, laborious, struggle. So, at a young age, I set up a subconscious program inside that said, "you must labor hard and struggle to prove you are worthy, otherwise you have no worth." As I laid on the couch for a month after the layoff, plunged deep into an identity crisis and feeling spent, depleted, exhausted and burnt out, I analyzed and second-guessed many of the steps I took during my climb up the ladder.

I knew from experience that self-reflection and growth is the only way out of being stuck in a negative, downward spiral of doom. Besides, becoming a true couch potato got old fast. But my stomach wretched at the idea of returning to a standard workplace because of the "me" it made of me. It also dawned on me once I stepped away from the office that work had replaced drinking in my life—I was of service to work first, before anything else. That realization underscored my sense that a traditional work environment was not going to be my next position.

A friend suggested I try my own business and pointed me toward an entrepreneur guru who specializes in Neuro-Linguistic Programming (NLP), a process to become more conscious of our subconscious minds. That awareness, which is cognizance of thoughts, gives us a chance to notice and change the unconscious programs that run all of us, which are built from a lifetime of experiences.

I began to dip my toe into this new approach and learned how to notice my thoughts. Internal confidence is based on the words I use to talk to myself, so was it any wonder that my internal confidence was low when the words I'd been using were so negative? The bare vulnerability exposed when the protective "false self-suit" was deconstructed by thought awareness made me squirm with discomfort. The harsh, denigrating words stung my being. I sensed that the negativity beast inside of me had a stake in keeping me playing small and second-guessing. I had negated accomplishments—figuring "you" (meaning anyone other than me) had achieved so much more, knew so much more, were better than me, etc. —and eroded my external confidence.

My spirit was depleted, and I was confused. I came face to face with a gaping disconnect—who I felt I was on the inside vs. who I looked like on the outside.

I needed to consistently change how I talked to myself. But how? As I captured thoughts the moment they occurred and I determined if those were the words I truly meant, I saw patterns emerging. One night on my way to a dinner party I had a huge realization—that my automatic, subconscious thoughts prioritized the needs of my kids, my friends, my family, my work—and not my own needs. This clarity hit me on the way to the gathering, as I began feeling stressed. I was running late, and I remembered that I needed to buy coffee because I ran out that morning. (One of the few things I do for myself is to begin the day journaling with a cup of coffee before anyone gets up.) Driving to the party I realized it was almost closing time at my favorite coffee place and I could feel my chest and neck tighten as I discounted my need—to get the coffee—and prioritized the "needs" of the party goers—to get there as soon as I could.

Because I had begun the work of being more aware of my thoughts, I felt the stress in my body and knew something was off. That awareness sparked me to pull over so I could pause, hear what I was saying to myself, and feel what was going on inside of me in that moment. My thoughts automatically subordinated my needs (the coffee) in deference to the "needs" of those at the party. Being consciously aware of my mind, I realized that wasn't true—the party goers did not "need" me—that was just something I told myself to keep me from caring for me. So, I chose to get the coffee, take care of me first, and be even later to the party. As soon as I made that decision, the stress and tightness dissipated, and I felt calm and quiet inside. When I ultimately got to the party, no one even noticed I was "late."

Something as simple as getting myself coffee was a huge turning point, as I could see for weeks and months afterward how my thinking about prioritizing others' needs thwarted and sabotaged much of my day. You put on your own oxygen mask first before helping others for a reason. Changing thoughts to kinder, more loving words wouldn't "stick" if I didn't also act toward myself with loving kindness in caring for my needs. This powerful insight, this "aha!' moment was seared into my brain: the congruency of prioritizing self-care along with using kinder, gentler words with myself were both required to grow consistent change in my thoughts.

And you know what? It worked! As I changed how I talked to and treated me, I changed how I spoke to and interacted with others. First, at home—my kids noticed. I was more present, less reactive and less of a taskmaster, asking more questions instead of making demands. The lines between my exterior and interior confidence blurred as I became more congruent—what I thought, what I said, and what I did became consistent.

As I caught my thoughts in the moment, discerned what I truly wanted to communicate to myself and changed my thoughts to words that more accurately described what I wanted/needed in the moment, I was treating myself with gentle care, which nurtured my being. It melted the hardness constructed to keep myself "safe" and I became kind, soft, and fluid to me, which made me softer to everyone else. Over time, I no longer felt "exposed" by the dismantled "false self-suit." Feeling vulnerable became more comfortable as my inner judge dissipated. I was transformed through this process: I stepped into my authenticity, my authority, my self-worth, my self-love.

Imposter syndrome disappeared, and authentic confidence grew. With inner congruity, my energy is no longer split between maintaining separate identities of what I look like on the outside and how I feel on the inside. In my full, congruent self I am unwaveringly confident, strong, firmly rooted, unflappable, unstoppable. I speak with truth and authority. My tone is steady and melodious.

This consistent strength and personal power fuels my passion to share my process—the path out of imposter syndrome, overthinking and second-guessing—with the rest of the world.

During this journey, I developed a four-step process that carried me from an insecure woman to the congruently confident person I am today. Before this journey to the center of me, I never could have imagined living in the calm peacefulness and ease I live in today.

So, what are the steps I took to become this confident, congruent, version of me that rarely analyzes and overthinks? Great question—one I wish I could have asked all those years ago.

The **First step** is to pause and become aware of what you are saying to yourself. What are the words? The tone? Is it your mother's chastising voice? Is it your vaguely disaffected "I don't care" voice? What kind of body language are you feeling as you think these thoughts? (I know that your "I don't care" voice comes with a shoulder shrug!)

You might balk and say, "How do I become aware of just one thought? My mind is racing all day long!" I'll reply: "Just start. Catch one thought!" TIP: It helps to put each of your hands alongside your face, next to your eyes, and focus your attention. You will catch a thought. That first time is all you need—because then you can set an intention to pay attention—and you will be aware of more and more thoughts. Said another way, you will wake up from your subconscious programs that are running your life.

At this point, some folks give up, finding excuses to stay the same because it feels too risky to change. They are comfortable in some areas of their life, and they don't want to sacrifice that comfort for a new kind of thought life that is unknown. This work does risk your current comfort zone. What is that comfort worth to you? There's no guarantee it'll always be there—I don't recommend waiting until those comfort zones disappear—poof! —with a lay off or some other unforeseen life event. Choosing this now, even a little, will begin to shift your mindset.

Second Step: As you hold that thought, observe what is happening. Hold each of your hands in the shape of an "o" and hold them up to your eyes as if you are looking through binoculars. Ask yourself questions, without judgment, about the language, tone and body language that you observe. Are these words accurately describing what you mean? Are you angrily chastising yourself? Catastrophizing a future event?

Third Step: Decide. Sit up straight and put your hand in a fist—like the "rock" in Rock, Paper, Scissors. Make a decision to use specific language with yourself, which brings more clarity to your thoughts. Experiment with changing them and feel how one different, upgraded thought can change everything—like a kaleidoscope turning, changing the entire picture by one small movement. Decide to choose the discomfort that comes from doing it differently and stick with it long enough to get past that feeling of discomfort. It will dissipate much more quickly when not fed with negative thoughts. Like a yoga pose—lean into the discomfort.

Now, don't be fooled. There can be a great chasm between deciding and acting—making the change. Don't give up now! You're almost there!

Fourth Step: Act. Get out on the stage of your life and change those thoughts. Practice the first three steps repeatedly—and allow yourself to make mistakes. Mistakes are wonderful learning opportunities. Have fun and play with it!

One of the great joys I discovered from doing this process repeatedly with myself, and now with my clients, is that it reconnects them to themselves, and a renewed sense of play and joy begin to spring forth. This can happen for you, too. When we're playful and joyful within ourselves, imagine the impact we make on those around us—our family, our friends, and folks we interact with every day.

If I can do this, anyone can! Take back your power and confidently choose your thoughts and choose your life—or someone else will choose it for you. Your future self will thank you.

Barbara Jenks

Barbara Jenks is a charismatic influencer known for navigating the dynamic landscapes of Fortune 500 and midsize companies, including Boeing and 20th Century Fox. During this journey, she has been recognized as a powerful trailblazer who has observed, mediated, and participated in countless interactions among executives and employees at all levels, solidifying her communication expertise. She founded Bright Fulcrum to share that expertise in simple, easy-to-apply techniques that massively transform how people and teams show up at work, home, and life.

Barbara's broad experience, blended with Neuro-Linguistic Programing techniques, empathy, and improv-inspired playfulness, empowers people to use clear and specific word choices, awareness and listening techniques to cut through the noise and fluff that cloud internal thoughts and interpersonal interactions. Her actionable tools and simple techniques reframe issues that keep people and teams stuck, freeing them to confidently make decisions and take action. Barbara's fun and practical mindsets give individuals, leaders, and teams the small shifts needed to massively change culture and enhance engagement.

Recognized for expertise in HR, Ms. Jenks is a Society of Human Resources Senior Certified Professional (SHRM-SCP), holds a bachelor's degree with distinction and maintains two certificates from Cornell University ILR school. In the community, Barbara regularly volunteers at a non-profit supporting victims of human trafficking and at a horse therapy stable.

Connect with Barbara at

https://brightfulcrum.com/coaching.

CHAPTER 2

Stay Rad

Becky Lapale

This chapter is dedicated to my family, friends, and recovering people-pleasers.

Have you ever been broken up with? And you were later thankful to the person who broke up with you? My experiences in life (the good, the bad, and the ugly) have shown me that everything really does happen for a reason. While you may not understand all the reasons why your life may change, with **reflection**, **acceptance**, and **discovering** what is next, those reasons will become clear.

Being a child of the '80s in southern California, I thought I'd share with you why "staying RAD" can help unblock you from the future. Whether it's personal or professional, being present is when doors open. Throughout this chapter, I'll be sharing with you an experience when my confidence wavered and how I rebuilt it. I have worked in corporate America for 20+ years (10 of them in big-tech). My professional career has provided opportunities for me to thrive and expand my awareness of who I am. Through adversities during my childhood, and my resilience in curiosity, I have figured out how to "stay rad" amidst the chaos. **Reflect**, **Accept**, **Discover** – without those three actions in place, you might lose sight of your priorities and what makes you smile.

Amazon

In 2024, I received feedback from my management team that I was not meeting the performance bar. My annual performance review came back titled *"Becky Lapale – Needs Improvement."* It felt like a swift punch to the gut. What do you mean I'm not performing? What about all the things I delivered for this company? That was my immediate reaction, followed by a wave of ego deaths for the weeks to follow. I felt betrayed, defensive, embarrassed, and hurt. With all these emotions at the surface, I took some time to delve deeper into why I was feeling that way. It was feedback, not a death sentence, so why was I taking it so personally? After countless hours of **reflection**, conversations with loved ones, tears, and a few therapy sessions, I arrived at **acceptance** and came to the same conclusion as my leadership. It was true. I wasn't meeting the performance bar.

How did I get here? What did I do wrong? The questions came pouring in on how to judge myself for how I got to that place with my leadership. The leadership I thought was inspired by me, the leadership that invested in me, the leadership that took risks with me, the leadership that now didn't approve of me. While I know this thinking is a bit dramatic, these are the thoughts that came flooding into my then very insecure brain. My confidence felt like someone had pulled a rug from underneath my feet. After seven successful years with Amazon, I didn't see it coming, and I felt blindsided.

The area I was underperforming was directly related to my leadership style not being in alignment with the company. I was told that my empathy was getting in the way of my next promotion, and that I would need to change to get to the next level. I was puzzled. I thought my leadership was what Amazon valued. I had an amazing team of experts who delivered above and beyond for our customers. We executed change management for three CEOs in four years and navigated the ambiguity in real estate during Covid. My team received multiple awards for our efforts in strategic planning, program development, and employee experience. I even received the Manager in Excellence award, so why was my leadership not a good fit anymore. It felt like everything the company had once celebrated about me was dismissed. My confidence was at an all-time low, and I needed to find out what was needed to help me regain my confidence.

That wasn't the first time I let Amazon influence my confidence. So why now did I want to prove my worth? Why do I care now? For a couple of years, I had been struggling to determine if Amazon was the right fit for me. Wasn't this what I had been looking for—another reason to leave and start something new? My values no longer matched the organization, so why was it so hard for me to leave? It wasn't until I questioned my confidence that I knew change was needed.

Reflect and Analyze the Data

The ending of a relationship (romantic or platonic) is one of the hardest things I think a person can experience. The normality you once knew is gone. Routines break, your confidence can waver, and everything around you starts to change. Just like in death, ambiguity in the unknown can feel heavy, emotional, and dark. Taking time to rebuild and restore yourself is important, but what to do first can feel overwhelming.

According to psychcentral.com, there are nine steps you can do to deal with the feeling of overwhelm. The first two are 1) **reflect** on the why and 2) **accept** your feelings. Whether it's someone breaking things off because they want to marry your best friend or whether a company doesn't value you anymore, both scenarios are difficult.

15

These experiences require you to **accept** the present and now **discover** how you want to move forward. When you need room to grow, something else must die. For instance, take the design of mushrooms. They digest dead matter around them so the soil can free up and make room for new plant life. When you prioritize time to **reflect** and let go of what doesn't serve you anymore, your "mushrooms" will have room to grow.

So, why am I under the performance bar? What feelings do I need to **accept**? What areas do I want to grow in? These are the questions I started to ask myself. My leadership gave me 60 days to decide if I wanted to start a new role or pursue something outside of the organization. To help me analyze, I looked back at where I started and how I got here. I needed more data to understand the why before making this decision.

I recalled how I grew up in the city of Orange, California. A conservative, old town feel with antique shops, awesome thrift store shopping, and of course orange trees. My family and I lived on "the other side of the tracks," the less traveled and poorer experienced part of Orange. I will admit, there was shame to where I lived. I would have people drop me off at a random house and then walk home because I didn't want them to know where I lived. The stigma that came from families who lived in my neighborhood crippled my confidence and I had to work hard at **accepting** my reality.

By my senior year in high school, I had moved out of my home and was renting a room. I paid $150 a month while making $7.50 an hour from my after-school job. Looking back (**reflection**), I'm impressed with what I accomplished in my youth. I took accountability for my decision to move out at a young age and **accepted** what was needed to succeed. I paid my rent, graduated high school, and **discovered** what was next. Into my young adult years, I continued to learn how to manage high-stress, disorganized, and chaotic situations (partially why I pursued a bachelor's degree in organizational management). I can

16

come into a room with a heated debate, reduce the noise, and leave with an action plan everyone has consensus on. The skillsets in this area definitively come from my upbringing. What I once ran away from as a child, was now the reason why I was good at my job; a "shaman of chaos."

Accept the Consequence and Be Open to Feedback

In July of 2018 B.C. (before Covid), I had been in weekly therapy for almost a year. I was on a 10mg daily anti-depressant, advancing in my career at Amazon, and had received my master's in organizational management. On paper I was thriving. I was a machine at my job, but it was all that I did. My health and personal life were being impacted because of my obsession with success. I was a workaholic, and I was blind to it. I knew the pace at which I was operating wasn't sustainable, but I convinced myself I was having fun.

The first time I walked into my therapist's office they politely asked, "So what brings you in today?" I replied, "I think I'm going to have a mental breakdown, and I'd like to prevent that." The therapist replied, "Ah, looks like we might have some control issues." I immediately became defensive and thought of all the reasons why they were wrong. I explained to them that I was laid-back, and a confident, non-controlling person. They politely smiled and said that they looked forward to getting to know this laid-back/confident/non-controlling person, who is about to have a mental breakdown.

There I was, at my first therapist session telling the expert they were wrong. The audacity and arrogance I had. Thankfully I was able to shift my thinking so I could actively listen more and judge less. It took me a little over two years to fully **accept** that I had control tendencies. My unconscious urge to "control a situation" was to prevent unwanted feelings and remain confident. Just like when I was 16, moving out of my home was an effort to help control the environment around me. I

17

discovered most results are only temporary and many things are out of my control.

At Amazon, I was managing a team that helped bridge culture (employee experience) and strategy (business development). To simplify, I brought the voice of the people bottoms up and negotiated with leadership direction top down. I became a respected professional in my industry and created dynamic team environments amongst my peers. It was my calling, and I was really good at it. I developed, influenced, and communicated key insights and future real estate planning across 60 businesses, 30+ locations, approximately 220k employees. I saved over 4 billion dollars in forecasted projects with future insights and predictive analytics in workplace behavior. The success in my career was a direct result of my ability to lead with empathy, and now I was being asked to reduce my empathy. This wasn't the first time I was asked, but I knew this needed to be the last. Being an empathetic leader is my superpower and it took me a long time to gain my confidence in that. After some **reflection**, I knew I didn't want to reduce my empathy, so, was me being under the performance bar a problem I had to solve? Or was it a difference in opinion I had to **accept**.

Discover Your Priorities and What Makes You Smile

During my path to **acceptance** with Amazon's feedback and where I was in my career, I had to slow down and peel back all the layers that created my belief foundation. To **discover** what actions needed to take place next, I had to go back and ask what my priorities were, and what I needed to do to get there.

> *"Studies show slowing down, being mindful, and experiencing and expressing appreciation will work. By doing it and focusing on it, neuroscience demonstrates new neural connections are made and strengthened…. As neuropsychologists are fond of saying, "Neurons that fire together, wire together." Over time, you'll find yourself happier, calmer, and experiencing more joy. It's science."*
> *~Psychologytoday.com (William Berry, 2015).*

When you understand what direction your priorities will take you, goals are established and accountability kicks in. Managing your priorities is key to a good routine and can boost confidence. You start to align your values with your personal and professional relationships. You remind yourself that you have all the power and it's up to you to make time to be present for it. When **discovering** what's next after a relationship ends, you need to leave the attachments behind of what you thought things should be, and free yourself from outdated mindsets.

It was 60 days since I received feedback from my leadership that I wasn't meeting the company's expectations. With a now lighter heart, clearer thinking, and my confidence back in place, I made the decision to leave Amazon. It was an end of an era, and I was excited to see what would grow in place of all the space I had allocated to Amazon. I let go of an environment that didn't serve me anymore and made room for new beginnings. I had the **reflective** evidence to **accept** that I had the skillsets to be successful outside of Amazon, I just needed the courage to **discover** what was next.

The day I communicated I was leaving the company, I received an accolade from a business partner. Accolades are a way for people to give public shoutouts when people go above and beyond. It was ironic really, but just more evidence that I am good at my job, and it's okay that I don't fit with the company anymore. The day before I left Amazon, I received an email with a note that filled my soul. It was another confidence reminder that I do have what it takes to continue to be a role model for others and I'm not finished with my work.

"Thank you for being such a constant and wonderful part of my growth at Amazon, not only as a role model of what it means to be excellent at your job and to hold yourself, others, and the company to a higher bar, but also as a shining light in the day-to-day." ~Anonymous

---

When You "Stay Rad," You'll Always Find Your Confidence.

If you ever lose sight of your confidence, go back and **reflect** on what helps remind you of your power. Challenges that come up in life are there to help you commit to your priorities, and if you pay close attention to what brings you joy, the unknown will become less scary. Below is a framework I used to help regain my confidence and embrace my power through this experience.

1. **Reflect** on your intentions.
   a. If good, how do you remind yourself of that?
   b. If not – find out why.
      i. How can you improve?
         1. What can you control?
2. **Accept** your consequence.
   a. How do you hold yourself accountable?
      i. Identify routine and goals.

3. **Discover** your priorities.
    a. What makes you smile?
        i. What does your smile maintenance look like?

Going through this framework can help reduce the noise and raise your confidence in what you are meant to bring into this world. I have seen success in this through my personal journey and professional experience in business planning. If you'd like to work with me in **discovering** what shifts are needed to help guide your future self, I'd love to offer a complimentary session to work with you. Just email me with the words "I want **RAD** Confidence." We will go through the framework and dive deeper into what you are looking to resolve.

Whether it's in business or personally, remember to stay rad and have fun with your future results!

Sincerely,

Becky Lapale lapale@gmail.com

PS – after I left Amazon, I sold my house, packed up my life in an 8x8x8 storage container, and decided to move back home to California. It was a cathartic decision and felt so right. I started my own business and ventured into entrepreneurship. The unknown was scary, but I made sure to pack my confidence with me. 😊

Becky Lapale

Becky Lapale has 20+ years of experience in workplace design, specializing in strategic planning, financial insights, and business development. She is an advisor who combines culture and strategy with class A problem solving, making the impossible possible.

With over a decade of working within big-tech companies like Microsoft and Amazon, Becky has made global impacts to future real estate workplace strategy, leading in program management, business partnership relationships, and predictive analytics.

Becky has a bachelor's and master's in organizational management, and raises the bar when it comes to emotional intelligence. Born and raised in Orange, California, Becky aspires to bring her authentic self and creative insights to people who are looking for more clarity in organizational management. Her "human first" approach in business partnerships creates the trust you need when planning for the future and she'll make sure you have fun in the process.

Connect with Becky on LinkedIn @beckylapale.

CHAPTER 3

Confidence Eats Experience, Skill and Knowledge for Breakfast

Catarina Bertling

To my grandmother Elin, who went for her entrepreneurial dream at a time when women didn't even have the right to vote. She broke the norm, and her unapologetic confidence is a true inspiration.

Five men all asked me the exact same question

I was at an elite soirée in a luxurious venue in Stockholm where wealthy investors and venture capitalists gathered together. After introducing myself as a Business Mentor for women, I got the exact same question from five different male investors - at different times.

"But Catarina, why are women so…. risk-averse?"

It's quite well-known that when men pitch their businesses to investors, many will do it with over-the-top confidence. With no hesitation, they will promise incredible returns, paint the picture of success beyond belief and world domination soon to come for their business. They sell their vision with absolute certainty, and it works.

Women often present with a more cautious approach. They strive to give a more truthful take on both the rewards and the risks of their business venture, and they seldom over promise the potential return of the investment.

Women also ask for a smaller investment from investors, thinking this is to their advantage.

Wrong.

This is perceived as a lack of confidence and makes the women seem risk-averse and insecure.

It goes without saying that women are just as driven and capable; it's just that their approach to conveying confidence is different.

The statistics speak for themselves, and the picture is very similar in the US and Europe.

- 1-2% of the big money goes to female founders. Yes, you read that correctly.
- 7 to 8% goes to founders of mixed genders.
- A staggering 90 to 92% is given to male founders.

This disparity in perceived confidence has a big impact that stretches far beyond the start-up world.

Whether you're seeking funding or just out to build a business that you're passionate about and can live well from, women need to build their confidence and project it outwardly.

Confidence is the cornerstone of success in selling anything to anyone. If you don't believe in your offers and yourself, who else will?

Confidence is crucial because it overrides experience, talent and knowledge. Every. Day. Of. The. Week.

Without confidence, even the most talented individuals struggle.

Confidence acts as a multiplier for your existing skills and knowledge and it amplifies your talents.

I say the biggest pitfall for female entrepreneurs is lack of confidence. So many women we've worked with doubt themselves. There are so many coaches/web designers/architects/fill in the blanks out there, so why would someone want to buy from me?

Interestingly, you would often not see lack of confidence and self-doubt from the outside. Many of our clients look very confident. They look like they've totally got their shit together and can look like a million bucks.

That tells you nothing - I repeat, nothing - about what's really going on inside of them. Looks really do deceive.

In our programs, it's not unusual that when the most confident looking woman in the room opens up and shares what's really going on, everyone is shocked as it turns out her business and life is nowhere near perfection. Instead, it's a mess.

So moving forward, when you see someone in real life (or on social media) that looks like they have all their ducks in a row - remember this:

"Never compare your own inside with someone else's outside." ~Catarina Bertling

---

Lack of confidence and self-doubt is holding so many women back from reaching their full potential.

So, what then is confidence, really?

What is Confidence?

The word confident comes from the Latin words con and fide. It literally means with faith.

Confidence is twofold: it's both an external and an internal affair. And it's all about trust.

External trust is how others perceive you. Many people around you—your family, friends, partners and clients—may think the world of you. They see you as reliable, competent, and trustworthy.

Internal trust is about how much you trust yourself, how you view yourself and how you value yourself.

Here is often where the real struggle lies.

Since childhood, people have confided in me their most intimate secrets. It happened again, recently.

I met a woman while traveling and we became friends. Despite having only met her twice, and only having had a few conversations with her, she shared with me a secret she had only ever told her best friend from high school.

This pattern of people trusting me has been repeated throughout my life.

However, despite this external trust, many of us often struggle with internal trust. Big time.

Why?

Simply because we really know ourselves.

Did you ever promise yourself that "Tomorrow I'll wake up early and start creating a healthy habit," and you were really confident and excited about it? If you're anything like me, you started out strongly setting goals to wake up at 5 a.m. every morning. You crushed it the first five days. On day six you decided you earned a little snooze, so you hit the snooze button. Again. And again. And again.

Or you decided to cut out sugar, only to find yourself indulging in a pint of ice cream two days later. (Swedes make the best ice cream. (Eat shit Ben & Jerry's.))

I would enthusiastically buy a gym membership … and never show up because I was too busy.

I have created plenty of proof that I can't be trusted! The lack of self-trust impacts every aspect of our lives. If we don't trust ourselves, there will always be a Trust Gap.

Understanding the Trust Gap is vital. It's that Gap between the outer trust and the inner trust; the Gap between how others see you and how you see yourself. The bigger the Gap, the more you will feel like a fraud. Because people will trust you, while you think, "If they only knew the real me…."

Imposter syndrome is a common thing with driven individuals. People doing really well in their corporate career have it. Entrepreneurs have it. Artists have it.

It's the feeling of "one day people will find out that I don't really know what I'm doing," "I may seem confident, but inside I'm doubting myself every hour. I'm scared the truth will come out."

True confidence starts within and there is no way that your lack of confidence will not show. It shows in the way you walk, in the way you talk, in your voice, and in the words you use.

So, if bridging the Trust Gap is this important, how can you do it?

From Panic to Success

It was the night before my big speech. I was set to enter the stage in front of 2,500 entrepreneurs from over 60 countries. I had rehearsed my speech for weeks before.

The evening before, I started the last practice round in front of the mirror. But the more I practiced, the more my heart sank. This was a five-day conference, and I was on the very last day. I had already listened to many speakers, and they were amazing. Brilliant. I started to compare myself. I realized that everything I wanted to say was probably already said. And said better. I started sweating, and felt the panic starting to creep in.

If I made a fool of myself on this big stage, I would never be hired to speak ever again—or at least that's what I told myself. There were event organizers in the audience looking for talent, for great speakers for their events and their stages. I would embarrass not only myself, I thought, but also the organizer if I got up on their stage. The audience traveled far and paid good money to learn from the speakers, and it would reflect really badly on the organizer if I spoke and revealed the nasty truth: I had nothing special to say. I was an amateur, a fraud.

So, there was clearly only one thing to do. I had to let the organizer know that it was in everyone's best interest that I withdraw. I decided I would get up early to tell them so they would have the chance to replan the schedule. With that thought, the stress eased and I fell asleep.

I woke up at 5:00 a.m.

I sat myself straight up.

I was filled with a powerful energy, almost out of this world.

"NO! THIS IS MY TIME!!"

Everything I had experienced, everything I had worked for—all my life's victories and defeats—had led me to this moment.

To be who I am.

And to be exactly where I'm supposed to be.

"I'm going to speak! I don't care if I fall flat on my face. I don't care if I deliver the absolute worst speech of all time. I simply don't care. It's my time now, and I WILL speak."

I gave myself only two tasks: to speak from the heart and connect with the audience.

I got up on that stage, and I rocked it.

I got multiple invitations to speak on other stages from people who heard me speak that day.

My speaking career took off.

My confidence totally failed me the night before. But in the morning I realized that all I needed was to believe in myself and make a choice - to trust myself and the journey that brought me there.

Boost Your Confidence!!

The good news is that you can boost your confidence. You can choose to take actions specifically designed to grow both your internal and external trust.

By actively making the choice to put myself on that big stage despite all of my doubts and fears, my confidence grew. I forever changed the way I see myself.

Nowadays, I am someone who is able to get up on a big stage and inspire thousands of people. I wasn't before. It came from a choice and a willingness to be uncomfortable and to risk failure.

Sometimes you get the chance to make a quantum leap in your confidence, like I did that day. But you can't wait around for those opportunities to present themselves.

What you can do is practice to choose confidence one step at a time by consciously choosing activities that you are slightly uncomfortable with. Don't wait until you feel confident; confidence grows with action.

The second thing that I invite you to do is to practice building your internal trust.

I would lie if I said it was a quick fix. Building internal trust takes time. It means keeping your promises to yourself, being consistent, and aligning your actions with your intentions. It's about proving to yourself that you ARE reliable, you ARE capable.

Start small. Make a small promise to yourself that no one else needs to know about. And then keep that promise. The next day, make another small promise to yourself. And keep that promise, too.

If you're anything like me, you have a lot of proof that in fact you are someone who breaks your promises to yourself. Your internal trust may be quite damaged. So please, when you practice this, be kind to yourself. Let it take time; let it be a process. But be in action. You get good at what you practice.

I'm a Business Mentor specializing in helping women grow and scale their businesses and their confidence so that they can live well from what they're passionate about - without selling their souls or compromising the quality of their lives. Women come to me for guidance when they feel stuck or overwhelmed and can't see clearly where they should focus and what the right strategy is for them.

I teach powerful business strategies to radically grow your revenue and freedom. Through our group programs, I've helped a big number of women throughout the years. I've seen firsthand how the lack of confidence stops women dead in their tracks from reaching their goals.

There are three key areas in your business where you absolutely cannot afford lack of confidence.

Confidence in Your Business

1. Confidence in selling is a big one!

Many women have a resistance or even sometimes a fear of selling. They don't want to seem pushy or salesy or disturb anyone, let alone face rejection. It's crucial for women to overcome that lack of confidence in sales.

Confidence allows women to trust their knowledge and instincts, enabling them to present themselves and their services with conviction and authenticity. Women who are confident in their selling abilities inspire trust and respect from clients, which leads both to increased sales and longer business relationships.

Ironically, many influential men that I meet agree that women are in fact not equal to men when it comes to sales - they are better!

2. **Confidence in setting prices** is essential for women entrepreneurs, but so many struggle.

Most women underprice themselves severely, leading to working long hours, unnecessary stress and suffering, and sometimes burn out. When women are confident in the value of their products or services, they can set prices that reflect their true worth without hesitation or apology. This confidence stems from a deep understanding of their expertise, the unique benefits they offer, and the true value for their clients.

Confidently setting prices also signals to clients that the service is high-quality and well worth the investment, building trust and respect.

3. **Confidence in being seen and heard** is crucial.

When we confidently showcase our skills, achievements and who we are, and position ourselves as experts and thought leaders in our fields, it changes the game for us. It empowers us to network effectively, engage with potential clients, and collaborate with powerful players.

Whether it's at a networking event, on social media or on a stage, you are missing out big time if your confidence is not in place. Your voice needs to be heard!

Finding My Passion

When I began my entrepreneurial journey, I originally intended to become a full-time angel investor.

I saw many startups lacking direction and risking failure. I was planning to move from being a passive investor to actively participating on the boards of directors and mentor the founders to succeed. The right guidance and support is crucial for so many startups.

As I spent more and more time in entrepreneurial circles, attending events with other angel investors and venture capitalists, I noticed something really odd. Where were the women? The massive male domination didn't make sense to me.

I knew so many talented, driven and extraordinary women with great ideas and potential - but they weren't being seen, heard or funded. That's when it hit me: my mission was to support these women. With my solid business background, I knew I could make a big difference.

Before starting my company, I had a successful corporate career where I achieved extraordinary results, significantly boosting revenue and profits in my marketing and sales roles. I studied at the Stockholm School of Economics (one of the world's top business schools) and built a vast network through my education and experiences. This network has been invaluable in connecting me with key players in different industries.

I've traveled the world for decades to learn from the best thought leaders and mentors.

My passion for growth and development has driven me to train and educate myself in many different modalities. I've deep dived in anything Business Building, Money and Personal Development, and sought out the most unique and transformative experiences. These experiences have shaped my understanding of what it really takes to truly succeed.

I bring a blend of hardcore business-building skills and a deep understanding of personal development and what it truly takes to build your confidence.

If you lack confidence and mindset, no amount of business skills and strategies will help. Conversely, if you don't have powerful business strategies, mindset alone will not be enough. Success requires both. The right mindset and the right business strategies - that works specifically for you. There's no one size fits all.

My mission is to inspire and empower more than 5 million women over five continents to create and execute a freedom plan for their businesses, their money and their lives - and to do it with confidence.

Key Takeaways

Bridging The Trust Gap

- Building confidence is a journey that involves both external and internal trust. It's about aligning how others see you with how you see yourself.

- By working on internal trust, you can bridge the Trust Gap and truly embody the confidence that others already see in you. Building inner trust starts with setting small, achievable goals and following through on your commitments.

- Confidence grows with action. So get comfortable being uncomfortable and consciously practice taking actions that you don't master to level up your confidence.

This essential transformation is not a quick fix, but when you truly start trusting yourself, everything is possible.

The 3 Key Areas:

Understanding and growing your confidence in these 3 areas is essential for your business success:

- **Sales** - if you're not comfortable selling, your business will struggle and so will you.

- **Pricing** - if you keep underpricing yourself, you will be forced to work long hours, and your clients will undervalue your contribution.

- **Being seen and heard** - if you can't show up with confidence, let your voice be heard and believe in yourself and the value you bring, you're setting yourself up for failure.

Valuing yourself and what you have to offer is fundamental to achieving success.

Confidence Is Essential: Confidence eats experience, skills, and knowledge for breakfast.

Is it unfair? Yes. Is it annoying? Absolutely. But it's the reality. You can debate it, yell at it or even start a movement against it, but the truth remains: confidence will win the race every single time. Confidence allows you to take bolder actions, seize opportunities, and inspire others. It's the driving force behind success.

Ultimately, when more women build their confidence and start to truly believe in themselves and the value they bring (and price accordingly!), not only do they boost their financial success. They also contribute to a culture that recognizes and respects women's contributions in business.

So make the choice today - I invite you to choose confidence!

Catarina Bertling

Catarina Bertling is Sweden's premier Business and Money Break-through Mentor and an International Award-winning Keynote Speaker.

With a degree from one of the world's top business schools plus 30 years of experience in Finance, Marketing and Sales, she is passionate about supporting women business owners to grow their business without selling their soul.

She is the creator of "The Bertling Method," a powerful 9-step method that helps women grow their businesses radically so that they can live well from what they are passionate about, without sacrificing the quality of their lives.

Her Mentorship Programs are highly sought after.

Catarina has been speaking at Harvard Club of Boston and Latin America's biggest business event SciBiz (with over 9,000 participants) and shared stages with the likes of:

Steve Wozniac (Co-founder of Apple), Mel Gibson, Christie Brinkley, Bret Michaels, Kevin Harrington (the original Shark from Shark Tank), John Travolta and Caitlyn Jenner, just to mention a few.

Her mission is to inspire and empower more than 5 million women to create and execute a freedom plan for their money, their businesses and their lives - and have fun while doing it.

She was born in Stockholm, Sweden, and drinks insane amounts of peppermint tea.

Connect with Catarina at

https://www.catarinabertling.com.

CHAPTER 4

Curiosity, Confidence, and Taking Your Seat at the Table

Colleen Kern

To my family and coaches: thank you for helping me cultivate a mindset that embraces the evolution from curiosity to courage to confidence.

The Golden Thread of Curiosity

Throughout my life, one constant has guided me through career transitions and health challenges: my insatiable curiosity. I've realized this curiosity is not just a personality trait—it's my superpower, the golden thread weaving through the tapestry of my experiences.

As a child, I approached the world with natural confidence, innately knowing everything would go according to plan. But at 14, chronic health issues began to chip away at that confidence. I still remember the first zing of shooting pain, doubling me over and sending me to the nurse's office. This marked the beginning of a life-long dance with chronic pain issues.

Despite my physical challenges, my curiosity remained intact, quietly influencing my decisions and ultimately leading me back to confidence. It became my lifeline, a way to engage with the world even when my body wasn't cooperating.

While confined to hospital beds as a teenager, I found solace in coloring books. The blank, white pages of sketchbooks felt overwhelming. However, the predefined structure of a coloring book offered a different kind of freedom. It provided an opportunity to create beauty within its parameters, using whatever energy I had that day. This early experience would later influence my approach to editing—finding beauty and meaning within existing structures.

Let Your Curiosity Guide You

When navigating your own confidence journey, consider this: What are you naturally curious about? What topics or activities draw you in, making you lose track of time? This curiosity can be your compass, leading you towards fulfilling work and renewed confidence.

My curiosity frequently precedes the courage to pursue unexpected paths.

Career Transitions: From Numbers to Words

My curiosity first led me to accounting—an unexpected choice for someone who loves words more than numbers. However, I was intrigued by its stability and curious about the stories hidden in financial statements. This curiosity allowed me to excel, even when I felt like I was faking it to make it.

As I entered my career, my curiosity to learn more often led to the courage to ask for new opportunities. My first job was with a regional accounting firm when they began transitioning to paperless recordkeeping. I loved it. It allowed me to push buttons in new software and see what happened. My curiosity to explore and see what happens was seen as the confidence to embrace new technology, leading to opportunities to work with transition teams.

My journey through the accounting world wasn't without its challenges. The long hours of public accounting (often requiring 60-hour weeks) weren't suited to my health. I'd don a mask, pretending everything was fine until I hit the point of burnout, often requiring hospitalization. This cycle of "faking it until I make it" wasn't sustainable.

Early in my career, I shifted into corporate accounting, hoping shorter hours and working for a single client would ease the cycle. However, the boredom was almost as bad. The novelty of the new challenges accompanying public accounting clients had helped fuel my curiosity, and confidence was now missing.

After being an accountant for seven years, I reluctantly got my CPA (Certified Public Accountant) license to improve my job prospects. I applied to one of the Big4 accounting firms, PwC, and to my surprise, I got a call for a contract position on a project I hadn't even applied for. However, when a Big4 calls you for an interview, you go.

My screening interview was scheduled while studying for my final CPA exam. I had so much information crammed in my mind for the exam I could barely remember my name. I was sure I had botched the interview, yet I moved forward. When I attended the in-person interview, I admitted, "I have no idea why I'm here." The position was in forensics, and up until that point, my experience was in corporate and large partnership tax accounting. Thankfully, one of the senior accountants took me under his wing and clued me into how valuable my tax expertise would be for this project.

It turned out the project was a contract position for the Deepwater Horizon Claim Settlement (BP Oil Spill) project. Transitioning to forensic accounting was a pivotal moment in my career – solidifying within me that our skills are often more transferable than we realize. My tax background, which I thought might be a limitation, was exactly what they needed to analyze and corroborate complex financial documents.

When faced with a career transition, whether by choice or circumstance, I find it helpful to approach it with curiosity. What new skills can you learn? How can your existing skills translate to this new field? Each transition is an opportunity to discover new strengths and build confidence.

Embrace Career Transitions as Opportunities for Growth

The Deepwater Horizon Claim Settlement project with PwC became the pinnacle of my accounting career. Here, my curiosity as to why they wanted to interview someone with a tax background for a forensics position, and saying yes to tan unknown opportunity, led to me transitioning from corporate tax accounting into forensic work. It came at a crossroad in my accounting career and required the courage and confidence to take a step down and to the side for the opportunity to work on one of the largest claim settlements in US history.

They needed people with strong tax backgrounds to decipher the various documents submitted. Throughout the four-plus years I contracted with PwC, I was challenged and expanded my critical thinking, technical writing, and analyzed claim documentation.

However, my favorite experience was the 18 months I was assigned to the Fraud, Waste, and Abuse team. I was one of three accountants from our team of 175 analysts assigned to the cross-vendor team to analyze fraud and work alongside experts from Wildlife and Fisheries, former FBI Directors, former military personnel, and a team of lawyers. Each day, I performed financial fraud analysis and wrote executive summary opinions so that they'd fit in an Excel cell using accessible, clear, concise language to be understood by the legal and management teams without accounting backgrounds—a skill that would prove invaluable in my future as an editor.

My confidence grew as I saw the value of my skills in this high-stakes environment.

Understanding Personal Strengths: The ADHD Revelation

It wasn't until I was 40 years old that I discovered I had ADHD. This diagnosis wasn't a setback—it was a revelation. It explained why my mind worked differently, why I thrived on novelty, and struggled with routine tasks.

Looking back, my ADHD likely contributed to my success in forensic accounting. The ability to hyperfocus on complex puzzles and see connections that others might miss were strengths I had long possessed but had yet to fully understand or appreciate.

Working with a mindset coach, we dove into my CliftonStrengths profile. My top strength? Learner. Of course—it all tied back to my curiosity! I wasn't flighty; I was a natural explorer, turning my "rabbit holes" of research into valuable resources for clients and friends.

This revelation was transformative. It helped me understand why certain environments and tasks energized me while others drained me. It allowed me to structure my work and life in a way that played to my strengths rather than constantly fighting against my natural tendencies.

Reframing my "weaknesses" meant recognizing that my tendency to jump from topic to topic wasn't a lack of focus but a sign of an agile, curious mind. My difficulty with routine tasks wasn't laziness but a need for novelty and challenge.

This reframing extended to how I viewed my health challenges. While chronic pain had often felt like a limitation, I began to see how it had made me more empathetic, more adaptable, and more appreciative of the good days.

What aspects of yourself have you been viewing as weaknesses? How might they actually be strengths in disguise? Understanding and embracing your unique attributes can be a powerful confidence booster.

The Seat at the Table: A Tale of Two Moments

Two pivotal moments in my career revolved around the concept of "having a seat at the table." The first was crushing. In a meeting at a new job, I shared my experience and suggestions. Afterward, a senior partner pulled me aside and said, "You're new here. You haven't earned your seat at the table. You're speaking up too much and making others uncomfortable. Stop talking until you've completed like 100 tax returns and have earned your seat."

This moment silenced me for a long time. It made me doubt my worth and my right to contribute. I began second-guessing every impulse to speak up, share an idea, or offer a different perspective. The confidence I had built through my experiences and successes seemed to evaporate in the face of this harsh judgment.

The second moment came years later, at a conference my marketing coach, Molly Mahoney, and I were both attending. By this time, I had left the accounting world behind and was exploring new career paths. Molly isn't just a marketing, AI, and organic sales genius; she's a caring friend.

Feeling out of place and not "cool enough" to hang out with successful entrepreneurs, I wandered away from those I considered "the cool kids." Molly noticed and later called me out on it. When I confessed my doubts, she emphatically stated, "You ALWAYS have a seat at the table!"

Those words hit me like a thunderbolt. Cue tears and a release from the old memory, from the limiting belief that I needed to earn my right to contribute. They reminded me that my voice, my experiences, my curiosity—all had value, regardless of my current title or years of experience in a particular field.

Claim Your Seat at the Table

Perhaps you also need a friendly reminder: you don't need permission to have a seat at the table. Your unique perspective, shaped by your experiences and curiosity, is valuable. Claim your seat with confidence!

This doesn't mean being brash or disregarding others' expertise. It means recognizing that your viewpoint has worth and that your questions and ideas can contribute to the conversation. It means being willing to speak up, even when you're unsure because sometimes the "naive" question is exactly what's needed to spark new insights.

Claiming my seat at the table meant embracing my diverse background. My experience in accounting, my journey with chronic health issues, my natural curiosity all inform my perspective and add value to my contributions.

Editing: Helping Others Find Their Confidence

Today, as an editor, I use my curiosity and confidence to help authors share their stories with the world. I'm not just polishing grammar or improving flow when I edit a manuscript; I'm assisting authors in seeing the value in their story and message, just as Molly helped me see the value in my voice.

My own experiences deeply influence my approach to editing. Just as I found freedom within the structure of coloring books during my hospital stays, I now help authors find their voice within the structure of their chosen genre or format. I see my role not as imposing rules but as helping authors infuse beauty and meaning within their chosen context.

I often tell authors, "Your story matters. Your message deserves to be heard. Let's work together to make it shine and share it with the world." This isn't just editing—it's empowering others to choose confidence in their voice and their story.

One of my favorite aspects of editing is seeing authors overcome their self-doubt and replace it with the confidence to hit publish. Many writers struggle with imposter syndrome, feeling that they're not "real" writers or that their stories aren't worth telling. I recognize these doubts because I've experienced them myself. Just as I once hesitated to call myself a writer, many of my clients hesitate to claim their identity as authors.

In these moments, I share parts of my journey. I talk about how I transitioned from accounting to writing and editing and learned to value my diverse experiences. I encourage them to see their unique backstory not as a liability but as a strength that gives them a distinctive voice that fuels authentic connection.

Your Story Matters

Whether you're writing a book or simply sharing your ideas via social media, remember that your story matters. Your unique experiences and perspectives inspire and help others. Don't let self-doubt silence you.

Recently, I shared my journey of navigating chronic health issues and career transitions in another book, culminating in speaking on the transformative power of boldly sharing our stories. The process of writing and publishing my story was both challenging and liberating. It required me to be vulnerable, to lay bare my struggles and triumphs for others to see.

The experiences reinforced a profound truth: we each hold the power to reshape our communities and become catalysts for change simply by boldly sharing our personal stories and truths. When we vulnerably share our stories, we tap into our shared humanity. It reminds us that we all face challenges, doubts, and triumphs. This openness creates compassion that fosters a sense of connection and understanding. Our stories create an emotional resonance that allows others to step into our shoes and perhaps catch a glimpse of themselves.

After the speech, audience members approached me, their eyes alight with recognition and relief. They thanked me for sharing my story, telling me how it resonated with their own experiences. One woman confided, "I never thought my struggles were interesting enough to talk about, but hearing your story made me realize that my experiences matter too."

This moment crystallized for me the true power of storytelling. By courageously sharing our truth, we create a space for others to gain the confidence to do the same. Even when our experiences differ, we can empathize with universal emotions of pain, loneliness, hope, and resilience. This authentic vulnerability is the birthplace of connection.

Moreover, I realized that this vulnerability is key to connecting with our ideal clients. As an editor, I work with authors who often struggle with self-doubt about their stories. By sharing my own journey, I demonstrate that I understand their fears and hesitations. I show them I've walked a similar path and emerged stronger for it.

By confidently sharing our stories, we're not just talking about ourselves—we're creating a space for others to see themselves reflected in our words. We build bridges of empathy and understanding by shining a light on perspectives and experiences that often go unheard or overlooked. This act of amplifying marginalized voices is a powerful catalyst for inclusion and change. Allowing others to see a reflection of their experience, helping them feel seen, validated, and less alone.

So, I urge you to embrace your story. Recognize that your experiences, no matter how ordinary they might seem to you, have the power to touch others. Your voice matters. Your journey matters. And by sharing it, you not only empower yourself but also inspire others to find the courage and confidence to share their own stories.

Remember, whenever you choose to speak up, write your thoughts, and share your experiences, you contribute to a larger narrative of human resilience and connection. You're showing others that they're not alone in their struggles and that there's hope on the other side of challenges.

Your story matters. Don't keep it to yourself. Share it and watch as it creates ripples of inspired confidence and change in the world around you.

Choosing Confidence Every Day

Confidence isn't a destination—it's a choice we make every day. It's choosing to be curious about ourselves and the world around us. It's deciding to see our unique attributes as strengths. It's choosing to courageously claim our seat at the table, even when others try to tell us we don't belong and own our story.

Some days, this choice is easier than others. There are still moments when I doubt myself when I'm tempted to shrink back rather than speak up. In these moments, I remind myself of how far I've come. I think of the young girl in the hospital bed, finding joy in coloring books. I think of the accountant who dared to ask questions and explore new areas. I think of the writer who finally claimed her identity.

As you navigate your confidence journey, remember:

1. Let your curiosity guide you. It's not just a trait; it's a tool that can lead you to new opportunities and insights.

2. Embrace transitions as opportunities for growth. Every new challenge is a chance to discover strengths you didn't know you had.

3. Reframe your "weaknesses" as unique strengths. Often, what sets us apart is exactly what makes us valuable.

4. Claim your seat at the table. Your perspective matters, even (or especially) when it's different from everyone else's.

5. Your story matters. Sharing your experiences can inspire and empower others in ways you might never anticipate.

And if you're struggling to find confidence in your own story, remember that sometimes we all need a little help to polish our words until they shine. That's what I do as an editor, and it's what we can all do for each other—help each other find the confidence to share our unique voices with the world.

Remember, when you choose confidence, you inspire others to do the same. And that's how we create a ripple effect of confidence that can change the world.

Ultimately, choosing confidence is about more than just feeling good about ourselves. It's about recognizing our potential to make a difference. It's about daring to believe that our voice matters, that our experiences have value, and that our story deserves to be told.

So, I encourage you to be curious, claim your seat, and tell your story. Choose confidence, not just for yourself, but for all who will be inspired by your courage to do the same.

Ready to confidently write your own story of transformation? Check out *The Ultimate Guide to Self-Editing Your Story of Transformation* (https://writeeditetc.com/self-edit) in the resource section.

Colleen Kern

With a knack for transforming written works, developmental content editor Colleen Kern helps subject matter experts and inspirational authors take their constantly rewritten drafts and turn them into published bestsellers. Alongside her love for editing, Colleen thrives on exploring new hobbies and knowledge, turning her diverse interests into valuable resources.

Connect with Colleen at https://writeeditetc.com.

CHAPTER 5

Living Beyond Fear - Unleash the Confidence That Is Already Within

Evakarin Wallin

With the "click!" of her mouse on the "buy now" button, Maria bought another business course. She hoped this one would be the tipping point, the missing piece that would finally make her marketing efforts successful. It wasn't the first time she had bought a course feeling this way.

She had big dreams; she envisioned creating a lifestyle where she could work from anywhere, making good money. She wanted to reach a point where she never had to worry about money again.

Maria had been in business for several years but hadn't seen the growth she hoped for. Many clients she has worked with in the past loved her work and she hoped they would spread the word. Unfortunately, very few did. She found herself scaling back her dreams, losing belief in their possibility.

"Who am I? Who would believe in me? Why would anyone want to hire me?" These were the thoughts that haunted her.

Maybe you've been there, too? Haunted by those same doubts and fears? Investing in course after course, program after program, and wondering why it's not working for you?

What no one tells you when you start your business is that knowing marketing strategies and sales training isn't enough to help you reach the big goals you've set and ensure your success.

No one tells you that you're embarking on a journey of facing your fears and challenging beliefs about yourself that you didn't even realize you had.

And no one mentions that when it feels heavy, when you're overwhelmed and stressed, it's not just about the situation you're in. It's how you respond to your feelings that will truly make the difference.

I'm sure you have heard many times that you can use the law of attraction to get what you want. You are always using it, always getting what you focus on.

Maria had an underlying tone of low self-esteem but also a big dream. Her dream is entirely possible for her to achieve, but only if she is willing to examine her unconscious beliefs that are running her life. It's impossible to make a good living doubting that people would hire her and value her service.

The good thing is that feelings of doubt give her (and all of us!) an opportunity to create awareness of what is running deep down and affecting business and life. And it also gives contrast.

The tricky part is that we have a part of our brain that doesn't want us to change. It's called the reptilian brain. No matter the situation, its purpose is to make us survive.

All of us have emotional wounds from childhood. Even if we had the best parents in the world, as children we interpret situations differently from how they are meant sometimes.

When a child experiences an event that is too emotional for it to handle, it will create a wound and get stored in the subconscious mind as a way to protect the child from having that traumatic feeling happen again. It makes it easier for children to survive. When we become adults, these wounds become our prisons if we do not take care of them.

Have you noticed that you run into the same situation over and over again, feeling the same kinds of emotions? That is a sign of a triggered wound.

Spending money on "bright shiny objects," like courses, tools, or programs you don't need right now is a way of addressing the feeling of "I'm not enough."

When you heal the wounds, they become your strengths. It can even become your superpower.

Let's dive into the nine most common wounds and their hidden superpowers. Do any of these sound familiar?

I am not perfect

The Wound - The belief is that you must be good and right to gain approval and love from others and yourself.

The Superpower - You develop high morals, make ethical choices, notice injustice, and have high standards.

I am not worthy

The Wound - You feel unlovable as you are and that you must be needed and indispensable to be loved and valued. You must meet the needs of others to earn love and validation. You are doing for others what you want others to do for you and there will come a point when you ask: What about me?

The Superpower - You are empathic and sensitive, an intuitive radar for perceiving the needs and desires of others. You can sense when someone requires support or attention, often offering help

51

before it's requested. You can pick up on unspoken feelings and offer comfort or assist accordingly.

I am not enough

The Wound - You feel that you are worthless or unimportant unless you are successful and appear admirable to others. You believe that you must achieve and succeed to feel worthy of love and respect.

The Superpower - You have an intuitive sense of what it takes to achieve your goals. You can easily see what steps and strategies are needed,

Your intuition guides you to present yourself effectively and you understand how to adapt and showcase your best qualities in various situations. You often possess an intuitive insight into market trends and consumer behaviors. You can make informed decisions about business and investments.

I don't belong

The Wound - You are a romantic and you believe that you are inherently different from others and marked by a unique, poignant depth of emotion. You feel isolated in your intensity and believe that you must hold onto your inner turmoil to maintain your distinctiveness.

The core belief is that you must continually express your individuality, creativity, and inner emotional landscape to be loved and appreciated. The romantic's identity is intertwined with the tragic beauty of life's complexities, and they feel the need to share this beauty with the world.

The Superpower - You have a deep, intuitive sense for recognizing authenticity. You can instantly perceive when something is genuine and when it lacks depth.

Your intuition leads you toward creative expression. You can sense unique avenues of self-expression and often produce original art, music, or literature.

You intuitively navigate your own emotions, understanding their intricacies. You are in touch with your emotional landscape and can often guide others through theirs.

I am not capable

The Wound - The unconscious wound here is the belief that you lack inner resources and must conserve your energy and knowledge to protect yourself from a demanding and intrusive world. You must possess knowledge and self-sufficiency to be secure and competent.

The Superpower - You possess an intuitive capacity for synthesizing knowledge. You can grasp complex ideas and distill them into understandable insights.

Your intuition enables you to grasp concepts intuitively, making connections between seemingly unrelated information.

You can easily become an expert in your field, driven by your intuitive quest for knowledge. You can delve deep into a subject and comprehend its nuances.

I am not safe

The Wound - You believe you are without guidance or support, making you vulnerable to danger and uncertainty.

You believe that you must seek security and guidance from authority figures to feel safe and protected.

The Superpower - you have an uncanny ability to sense potential threats and challenges. Your Intuition guides them in anticipation of potential dangers.

Your intuition aids them in evaluating situations for potential pitfalls and dangers, making them cautious and prepared.

You intuitively detect whom you do not trust. You rely on your intuitive sense to enhance the abilities of those around you.

I am not allowed to be sad

The Wound - You believe that you are deprived or in pain and you must escape discomfort and suffering to find happiness and fulfillment.

You must seek pleasure and avoid pain to be content and free.

The Superpower - You are intuitive in spotting opportunities and possibilities and can identify potential adventures, endeavors, and exciting prospects.

Your intuition guides you in creative endeavors. You can intuitively see how to turn your visions into reality.

You possess an intuitive knack for adapting to new situations. You can quickly navigate change and embrace diverse experiences.

I am powerless

The Wound - The unconscious wound is the belief that you are vulnerable and must be strong, assertive, and in control to protect yourself and those you care about.

The core belief is that you must be powerful and responsible to be respected and secure.

The Superpower - You are highly intuitive in your understanding of power dynamics. You can assess authority and control in various situations.

Your intuition guides you in understanding how to influence others, and you can assert your authority effectively.

You possess an intuitive drive to protect and empower those you care about. You can sense when your loved ones need support and act on it.

I am nobody

The Wound - The unconscious wound is the belief that you are disconnected or in conflict with others and the world, and you must maintain peace and harmony to avoid conflict and discomfort.

The core belief is that you must maintain inner and outer peace to be valued and loved.

The Superpower - You have an intuitive sense of detecting underlying conflicts and tensions. You can sense when disharmony is present.

Your intuition guides you in mediating conflicts and bringing unity to a situation. You intuitively understand how to restore tranquility.

You possess an intuitive knack for facilitating peaceful cooperation. You can sense when collaboration is needed and help bring people together.

Maria's experience could have been mine.

I've too often purchased a course I believed I "needed" for later, lured by a deal that seemed too good to pass up today.

Each emotional wound takes us further from our true selves, diminishing our confidence.

When we feel out of place, we search for a sense of belonging, yet it always seems elusive. Even when welcomed into a group, we may still feel like outsiders or, worse, find ourselves unwelcome.

These beliefs operate silently in the background, surfacing when we are triggered.

You cannot heal your wounds by merely changing your thoughts; you must move beyond the logical mind, beyond analyzing, and release the need to understand the origins of these beliefs.

Being triggered offers a golden opportunity to gain awareness and initiate change.

My deepest wound was feeling like "I am nobody." This led me into conflict-ridden relationships where I felt unlovable and suffered from low self-esteem. It felt as though there was a war inside me, affecting my daily life making me yearn for peace.

My journey involved confronting the parts of myself I was afraid to feel. It was painful to feel lesser than others, and I couldn't see why anyone would want to be with me. I also felt as though I was a problem for others.

My path from being stuck in my wound to stepping into my superpower started when I attended a party where I felt I didn't belong. I was completely out of place, and I suspected no one would have noticed whether I was there or not. I waited until it seemed appropriate to excuse myself and leave.

When I got home, I could no longer ignore the familiar knot in my stomach. I took out a pen and paper and started journaling. I asked questions about the pain, asking what it wanted from me and why it was present.

And I received answers. They told me that I didn't belong, that I shouldn't try to fit in with these people because they were better than me, and that I should stick with my own kind.

I continued writing, even though it was painful to confront these thoughts on paper. I knew I couldn't run from it any longer. And suddenly, the pain dissipated. And I felt good. I no longer felt unworthy. Looking out the window, I saw the trees and houses outside. They were the same, yet they appeared different.

It was I who had changed.

That was the day I fell in love with fears and challenges.

The process of releasing these feelings led me to peace. From that day on, I sought the simplest and most profound ways to dissolve and transform fears and obstacles. It took a few years before The Expansion Method was created. That was in 2010. I incorporated it into my coaching, and it became a success.

Since then, I have helped thousands of people transform their relationships with themselves.

As business owners, we want to make money. But too often I hear people say: "I want to make enough money so I never have to worry about it again." This is a misconception. Worrying about money only leads to more worry about money. Even if you accumulate a fortune, the worry doesn't simply disappear. You might worry about losing it, how to invest it, or who to share it with.

Releasing worry and fear liberates you. Behind these feelings lie trust in life and openness to what comes next, and then life truly begins to flourish.

1. **Think about what you desire**. Choose a specific goal. Imagine that you have already achieved it and notice how good it feels.

   Don't aim too big or too far into the future. It doesn't mean you can't achieve a substantial, ambitious goal. If it's too large, you might not connect with it emotionally, which is necessary to propel you forward. If you're unsure about the steps to take today toward this big goal, break it down into smaller, more manageable goals.

   Feeling a mix of inspiration and doubt is a good sign—it means you're being realistic about the challenges ahead.

2. **Consider the worst-case scenario**. What is the worst that could happen? Understand that this is just one of many possible outcomes. Dig deep and don't stop at the first answer. For each response, ask yourself, "What's the worst thing about that?" Continue until you can think of no further answers.

3. **Accepting this scenario is crucial**. Fear of the outcome can keep you stuck. Acceptance is powerful; it calms your nervous system and diminishes the fear's hold over you.

   Forgiveness is a vital tool here. Instead of directing it towards others, turn inward. You possess everything needed for transformation within yourself.

   Place your hand on your heart and say, "I forgive myself for believing..." followed by the specific fear or limiting belief you identified. Repeat this until you truly accept the forgiveness.

4. **Now, liberated from unconscious fears, revisit the positive feelings associated with achieving your goal**. Spend some time relaxing and daydreaming. In a relaxed state, your subconscious mind is more receptive, especially just before sleep and first thing upon waking.

    Enhance this process by doing something joyful or fun just before you relax and visualize your success. Happiness accelerates your ability to internalize positive outcomes.

5. **Close your eyes and consult your intuition**: "What action do I need to take to create this outcome?" Do what your intuition tells you to do, even if you cannot see the benefit logically. You will be amazed at how you will start experiencing that you are at the right place at the right time.

Connect with your intuition, which holds all the answers. Intuition might subtly nudge you, provide images, or even words—it's a brief but genuine knowing.

If fear or doubt accompanies these intuitive signals, they're likely not true intuitions. If you're new to this, be patient and practice; it takes time to strengthen this 'muscle.'

You are more powerful than you might think. Living beyond fear is magical. Nature is searching for life and growth everywhere. Be like nature and instead of making choices based on fear and limitations, make them based on growth, learning to trusting yourself in the process.

Your current situation is the result of your past choices and actions. By fully accepting responsibility, you empower yourself to reshape your reality.

I am continually amazed at how every person has a unique story, yet we are all profoundly similar. We experience the same emotions, share similar wounds, and we're all in pursuit of feeling good.

The journey to feeling good and confident lies in accepting ourselves as we are. It's a beautiful process to peel away the layers of beliefs that prevent you from expressing your true self.

True freedom comes from releasing the limiting beliefs about who you are. You reclaim the innocence of your childhood, now enriched with the wisdom you've gathered along the way. This transforms you into a powerful creator, capable of reshaping your life repeatedly and enjoying the journey you've been granted.

When you release fear and worry and start to trust in yourself and life, you'll notice magical shifts in your external reality.

New opportunities will emerge, and you'll confidently embrace them, feeling deserving of these experiences and enjoying the world you've crafted for yourself.

Evakarin Wallin

Are you ready to choose a bigger, better life for yourself? To never to be stopped by your fears, frustrations or overwhelm? Evakarin Wallin is the Founder of The Expansion Method and on a mission to share with business owners how they can step into their confidence and create Fearless Success.

Through finding the obstacles that stand in the way of you creating the life and business you want, you can be empowered to shift outdated beliefs and ideas, and quickly and effortlessly move forward towards your ultimate desires. Evakarin's proven techniques allow anyone to easily increase their confidence, show up at a new level and attract bigger and better opportunities.

Known internationally as the Queen of Transformation, she helps her audience and clients release what is holding them back and rewire their minds so they can easily step up their game and grow their business. Best-selling author of *From Inner Limits to Outer Success*, Professional Speaker, she has been a featured leading expert on national and international platforms.

With more than 20 years of experience of working with amazing clients, Evakarin has a track record of guiding them to achieve remarkable success. Her mission and commitment are to teach you how you can take any obstacle you face and transform it into a possibility, making it easy to take action and achieve your goals.

To learn more about Evakarin Wallin and Living Beyond Fear, you can find her at evakarinwallin.com.

CHAPTER 6

From Vision to Victory: Transforming Lives with Purpose and Technology

Joy S Francis

I dedicate this to my husband Jim, whose unwavering support has been with me every step of the way as I spent countless hours writing and developing programs.

Have you ever wondered how to turn challenges into triumphs or transform adversity into a beacon of hope and success? My story does just that in a world where technology and human potential intersect.

Welcome to a journey spanning decades, marked by determination, resilience, and an unyielding quest for purpose. I'm Joy Francis, and my path has been paved with obstacles—being blind since birth was just the beginning. This challenge ignited a fire within me to help others see the possibilities in their lives, literally and figuratively.

My career began in the bustling heart of corporate finance, where I navigated the highs and lows and witnessed firsthand the profound impact of ineffective sales processes. These experiences fueled my passion for crafting better solutions. Moving into teaching financial management and business development, I saw the transformative power of knowledge and the critical role of technology. One question always drove me: What makes people buy, engage, remain loyal, or walk away?

Imagine a tool that doesn't just organize your contacts but becomes an integral part of your sales team. I set out to create that with RevTurbo™ CRM—a revolutionary approach blending the latest AI technology with the timeless touch of human connection. This isn't just another piece of software; it's a game-changer designed to meet the unique needs of every business.

In this chapter, you'll discover the pivotal moments that shaped my journey and the transformative power of finding your purpose. From helping small businesses thrive to empowering women to achieve financial independence, every step has reinforced a simple yet profound truth: when you succeed, we all succeed.

Join me as we explore how embracing your power and leveraging technology can lead to a legacy of confidence and lasting impact. This is more than a story; it's a blueprint for anyone ready to transform their life and the lives of others. Let's embark on this journey together— from vision to victory.

May the profits be with you, Joy Francis, CFO and AI Automation Strategist.

Helping Small Businesses

At the age of 31, I found myself at a crossroads. After successfully navigating a mortgage company out of bankruptcy, I was fired during a family squabble. But with extensive banking knowledge, I didn't stay down for long. I became a sought-after expert in writing loan proposals and grant requests, catching the attention of several Small Business Development Centers (SBDC) in Metro Detroit and a Detroit Venture Capital Group.

The US Small Business Administration (SBA) established the University Small Business Development Program in 1976 to counsel and train small business owners. By 1980, it evolved into the SBDC, which continues to assist small businesses today. Whenever clients needed a loan, I was their go-to person. Over the years, I helped numerous businesses secure bank loans and venture capital, guiding them through the often complex process of obtaining financial support.

One of my favorite clients was a doctor and his wife, who developed the left ventricular assist device (LVAD). This doctor taught me to never accept "no" as the answer. Similarly, the CEO of the mortgage company had instilled in me the philosophy, "When someone says no, your response is, how can we make it work?" Combined with my mother's words, "You can do anything if you set your mind to it," these lessons laid a clear path for me.

Combining the teachings of these two remarkable gentlemen with my mother's wisdom, I learned that perseverance is key to achieving anything. We each have a unique gift, something truly special that only we possess. My higher power, whom I call God, has blessed us with these gifts; it is our responsibility to share them with the world.

While there may be few Einsteins among us, we all have a unique gift. For me, that gift is my blindness. Not being told about my condition until my 30s, I never learned to be blind in the conventional sense. I received a BS in accounting and an MBA with a concentration in finance without ever being able to read a page out of a book.

I found ways to navigate, see, and achieve things doctors told me were impossible. This unconventional approach to my blindness allowed me to develop a perspective and set of skills that were uniquely my own.

My mother always said I could do anything, and I believe it wholeheartedly. If you didn't have someone to tell you that, please accept my mother's words or mine: you can do absolutely anything if you set your mind to it. Does that mean you can lift a 400-pound barbell right now if you weigh 90 pounds? Only if you've been training for it. But with dedication and effort, you can build the strength needed to achieve such feats.

In the early 1980s, I had the privilege of meeting W Mitchell. In 1971, he survived a cable car accident that burned over 65% of his body. In 1975, he co-founded Vermont Castings, later valued at $65 million. Despite a plane crash in the same year that left him a paraplegic, Mitchell's spirit remained unbroken. In 1997, he published a book that still resonates with me: "It's Not What Happens to You, It's What You Do About It." His story is a powerful testament to the resilience and the power of the human spirit.

Mitchell's story profoundly impacted me. His ability to overcome such tremendous physical challenges and still achieve remarkable success reinforced my belief that we all have the potential to triumph over our obstacles. It reminded me that no matter what life throws at us, we can choose how we respond and keep moving forward.

Throughout my career, I have seen the transformative power of this mindset in action. By helping small businesses secure the funding they need to grow and thrive, I witnessed firsthand the impact that perseverance, resourcefulness, and a positive attitude can have. These experiences solidified my commitment to helping others and fueled my passion for finding innovative solutions to businesses' challenges.

Working with the SBDCs and the venture capital group, I saw the tangible results of my efforts. Small businesses that started with just a dream and a loan application went on to become successful enterprises, creating jobs and contributing to their communities. This work was not just about numbers on a balance sheet but about making a real difference in people's lives.

No matter what challenges arose, I continued, echoing my mother's words: "You can do anything if you set your mind to it." This mantra has been my guiding light, helping me push through difficulties and strive for excellence.

As I continued assisting businesses, I realized that my role was more than providing financial expertise. It was about empowering others to believe in their potential and pursue their goals confidently. Whether it was a new startup seeking its first loan or an established business looking to expand, my mission was to help them see beyond their immediate challenges and envision a brighter future.

In this way, I have helped businesses secure the financial support they needed and instilled in them a sense of resilience and determination. By sharing the lessons I have learned and the strategies I have developed, I hope to inspire others to embrace their unique gifts and overcome any obstacles they may face.

Helping small businesses has been one of the most rewarding aspects of my career. Each success story is a testament to the power of perseverance and the impact of a supportive community. It reminds me that, no matter the journey's difficulty, there is always a way forward if we remain committed to our goals and believe in our abilities.

As you read this chapter, I invite you to reflect on your journey and consider how to use your unique gifts to make a difference. Remember, you can do anything if you set your mind to it. Let this be your guide as you navigate the challenges and opportunities that lie ahead, and may you find the strength and determination to achieve your dreams.

Teaching and Mentoring

My success with the SBDCs led various colleges and universities to notice how much I was helping business owners. The University of Detroit Mercy invited me to teach Managerial Accounting in their Master of Engineering Management program. Other local colleges asked me to develop training programs and teach small business classes.

After teaching my classes at Ford Motor Company for a few semesters, the boss hiring the college asked me to help him. He needed help getting the college to complete the work needed to offer their classes. He asked me to get the UAW-Ford Center's approval to offer my classes directly to their employees.

The college wanted to retain the tuition but was as frustrated as the Ford employee. Therefore, it agreed that I should offer my classes directly to the Ford employees.

As the years passed, each new Education Training Coordinator asked me to create new financial management and business development training. This led me to create 18 certified small business training programs for UAW workers at Ford Motor Company. Teaching was challenging—one day, I was instructing students at an engine plant in Metro Detroit; the next, I was teaching a different course at an assembly plant in Norfolk, Virginia.

Most people had one of two questions about their business: "How do I make more sales?" or "How can I keep more money for myself?" With my financial background, answering the second question was easy. I developed a system to teach people how to save more money, creating another course to get certified. This new class taught people how to pay off all their debt, including their mortgage quickly.

But I continued pondering, "How do I make more sales?"

Empowering Women

Teaching people how to repay their debt quickly felt almost like magic. Most of my students were women. One night, while praying, I felt a calling—a deep, resonant directive to assist at least 1 million women in making and keeping more money. That moment was a turning point, crystallizing my mission and setting me on a path to make a significant impact.

To understand the power of becoming debt-free, we first need to address what fuels the desire to pay off debt. The goal will likely only be achieved if the desire is rooted in doing it for yourself. True success in becoming debt-free starts with a personal decision. The desire must come from within, driven by a commitment to oneself. Once you decide to become debt-free, the process is simple but challenging. Like anything worthwhile, it requires dedication, sacrifice, and a willingness to change ingrained habits.

Over the years, hundreds of people have chosen to follow my debt-free program. While this number is substantial, it has yet to be the million women I was directed to assist. This calling continues to drive me, reminding me that much work still needs to be done. Each person who becomes debt-free reignites the fire in my soul, motivating me to reach out to more and more people.

Teaching women how to run a business, make money, and pay off their debt was a crucial start. However, I soon realized that more was needed to answer the first question about making more sales. Understanding the mechanics of sales and the psychology behind buying decisions became my next focus.

Women often face unique challenges in the business world. Traditional financial advice and sales strategies sometimes overlook the nuances of women's experiences and needs. Recognizing this, I tailored my programs to address these specific challenges, offering financial guidance and the tools and strategies needed to excel in sales.

Empowering women means equipping them with the confidence and skills to navigate a competitive business landscape. It's about breaking down barriers and providing support systems that foster growth and success. One of the most rewarding aspects of my work has been witnessing the transformation in my students. Women who once doubted their abilities now lead successful businesses, confidently managing their finances.

As I continue to develop and refine my programs, I remain committed to assisting at least one million women. Each success story brings me closer to this target, providing motivation and validation. The journey has been filled with challenges, but the rewards far outweigh the obstacles.

Empowering women is not just about financial independence; it's about transforming lives and creating ripple effects that benefit entire communities. Women who achieve financial stability and business success often reinvest in their families and communities, multiplying the impact of their achievements.

The stories of transformation fuel my passion and commitment. Every woman who achieves financial independence and business success becomes a beacon of hope and possibility for others. The cumulative impact of empowering women is vast, creating a stronger, more equitable society.

As I look forward, I remain focused on expanding my reach and refining my programs to meet the evolving needs of women in business. The journey continues, and with each step, I move closer to the goal of assisting at least one million women. The mission is clear, and the path is laid out. Together, we can achieve financial independence, business success, and a legacy of empowerment for future generations.

Teaching them how to run a business, make money, and pay off their debt was a start, but more was needed to answer the first question about making more sales.

Creating RevTurbo™ CRM

Finance is different from sales and marketing. Over the years, as I immersed myself in learning marketing concepts and teaching sales courses, I became acutely aware of a significant problem. Only 3% of your audience is ready to buy what you are selling at any given time.

This statistic was a revelation. It explained why many businesses struggled with sales despite having excellent products or services. Most salespeople follow up at most three times before giving up, losing potential customers who might have converted with a bit more persistence. The question that haunted me was: "How can we help more business owners make more sales?"

The answer came to me through a blend of technology and human insight. Imagine a tool that doesn't just organize your contacts but becomes an integral part of your sales team. This vision led to the creation of RevTurbo™ CRM—a revolutionary approach that blends the latest AI technology with the timeless touch of human connection. This isn't just another piece of software; it's a game-changer designed to meet the unique needs of every business, providing them with a competitive edge in an increasingly complex marketplace.

Creating RevTurbo™ CRM was about developing a new tool and transforming how businesses approach sales. Everyone has a unique and special gift to share, and I believe that RevTurbo™ CRM must also be unique.

The typical one-size-fits-all approach needed to be revised. My unique ability to see things most cannot helped me develop a program that answers the critical questions of what, why, when, how, and where a prospect will buy. Using artificial intelligence, I created a system that predicts when a prospect will most likely make a purchase.

The journey to develop RevTurbo™ CRM delved into behavioral psychology to understand what drives customer buying decisions. This research phase laid the foundation for a system that could integrate advanced technology with deep human understanding.

One of the key insights from my research was the importance of timing in sales. While traditional CRM systems could track interactions and manage contacts, they do not predict when a prospect would be ready to buy. Artificial intelligence could significantly fill this gap. By analyzing patterns in customer behavior, AI could identify the optimal times to reach out to prospects, increasing the likelihood of a successful sale.

Another critical element was personalization. Generic follow-ups and sales pitches are often ignored because they don't resonate with the prospect's unique needs and circumstances. RevTurbo™ CRM is designed to provide tailored recommendations, helping sales teams create personalized engagement strategies. This personalization is achieved through sophisticated systems considering various factors, including past interactions and demographic information.

The RevTurbo™ CRM system provides actionable insights, helping sales teams focus their efforts where they are most likely to yield results.

RevTurbo™ CRM has also been a powerful tool for empowering entrepreneurs. Many women-led businesses have unique challenges and perspectives, and the system's ability to provide personalized, data-driven insights has been particularly beneficial. By helping these businesses succeed, RevTurbo™ CRM contributes to broader economic empowerment and gender equality.

Looking ahead, RevTurbo™ CRM's potential is vast. Integrating emerging technologies like natural language processing and sentiment analysis could further enhance its capabilities. Imagine a system that predicts when a prospect is ready to buy and understands the emotional tone of their communications, allowing for even more personalized and effective engagement.

The journey to create RevTurbo™ CRM has been one of the most fulfilling aspects of my career. It combines my passion for technology with my commitment to helping businesses succeed. This tool embodies the philosophy that sales are about transactions, building relationships, and understanding human behavior. As more businesses adopt RevTurbo™ CRM, I am excited to see the positive impact it continues to have, helping companies thrive and achieve their full potential.

RevTurbo™ CRM is more than just a tool; it is a testament to what can be achieved when technology and human insight come together. It is designed to empower businesses, enhance sales processes, and, ultimately, help more business owners make more sales.

Legacy of Confidence

No matter how much I wish I were the only abused child, many children grew up with a parent telling them that everything they did was either wrong or not good enough. My father was the abuser, but my mother was always there telling me, "You can do anything if you set your mind to it."

Empowering others through technology has reinforced my confidence. The broader impact of AI-driven solutions on global business landscapes is immense. I encourage you to find your purpose and empower others using modern tools. Let's embark on this journey together—from vision to victory.

Joy S Francis

Joy S Francis, CFO and AI Automation Strategist, has been blind since birth. Since 1984, she's made her mark as an international best-selling author, speaker, and trainer, making a significant impact by helping over 20,000 people start, grow, and exit their businesses.

Joy's journey is far from ordinary. With hands-on experience steering companies through tough times, she saw firsthand the damage inefficient sales processes can cause, fueling her quest for better solutions.

Believing in the power of tailored approaches, Joy created RevTurbo™ CRM. This innovative tool reflects her deep experience and passion for problem-solving, meeting the unique needs of every business.

Get Your Path to Untapped Profits at

https://www.joyoussuite.com/request.

CHAPTER 7

Confidence Is the Journey to Freedom

Karen Vaile

To Sue, my wife and partner: You've been my greatest fan, unwavering cheerleader, and solid rock throughout my journey of growth and development. This book is dedicated to you with all my love and gratitude for your constant support and belief in me.

Standing in the doorway, I felt a surge of panic threatening to overwhelm me. The possibility of passing out or becoming sick loomed ominously, adding insult to injury and fueling my fear of embarrassment. On the surface, the task at hand seemed simple enough – extend a hand and greet those entering the room. But as anxiety gripped me, I realized just how daunting even the most seemingly mundane interactions could be. With a heavy heart, I abandoned my post and retreated to the safety of the washroom, seeking refuge until the meeting commenced.

At 22 years old, one might have assumed that quitting alcohol would have ushered in a new era of improvement in my life. However, the reality was far from that hopeful expectation. Instead, I came to the startling realization that alcohol had been my crutch, providing me with a false sense of bravery to tackle the daily responsibilities of adulthood. From mundane tasks like going to work, brushing my teeth, and running errands to more social activities such as chatting with coworkers or calling my parents, alcohol has been my silent companion, bolstering my confidence in the face of life's challenges. Yet, this facade of courage came at a steep cost – each night was spent in a haze of intoxication, only to wake up and repeat the cycle once more.

Upon awakening, I was greeted not by the peace of a new day, but by violent tremors coursing through my entire body. It wasn't the physical manifestations of withdrawal that haunted me now – those were a thing of the past. Instead, it was an overwhelming sense of anxiety and fear that gripped me, rendering me powerless in its wake. My mind raced at a frenetic pace, a whirlwind of thoughts swirling chaotically, impossible to grasp. It felt as though a legion of squirrels had taken up residence in my head, their incessant chatter drowning out any semblance of coherence and even more impossible to focus. In the face of such overwhelming turmoil, alcohol had become my crutch, offering a temporary escape from the crippling anxiety that made even simple tasks, like saying hello to someone, seem insurmountable.

As the months passed and I remained committed to sobriety, I found myself facing an unexpected challenge: the worsening of my anxiety. My hands trembled incessantly, and I became hyper-aware of every public restroom, planning my activities around easy access. The anxiety took a toll on my physical health as well – I couldn't eat, and the weight loss was so drastic that my family feared for my well-being, mistaking me for someone suffering from a serious illness. Despite my efforts to push through the fear, it seemed to intensify with each passing day, leaving me in a constant state of terror with no clear understanding of its cause. Eventually, I realized I couldn't navigate this battle alone and sought professional help.

They gave it a name: Social Anxiety Disorder, and that's what I was diagnosed with. I was prescribed medication to help manage the overwhelming feelings it brought. Essentially, it's an anxiety disorder characterized by an intense fear of being scrutinized and judged by others, to the extent that it disrupts daily life. Simply put, it's Fear of People's Opinions (FOPO). Somehow, assigning it this acronym, or even referring to it as SAD (Social Anxiety Disorder), helped strip away some of the stigma and powerlessness associated with the clinical term. I realized that while I could handle interactions over the phone or one-on-one, adding just one more person to the mix often made it unbearable. Everyday activities like eating lunch with coworkers or using public restrooms became monumental challenges. I felt like an outsider, different from everyone else. But the most troubling realization was that my fear stemmed not from what others thought of me, but from what I thought of myself. My lack of self-esteem and confidence fueled a vicious cycle of self-judgment and perceived judgment from others. I knew that the real remedy was building up my confidence, rather than relying on medication.

What followed was a journey of about 20 years, characterized by sporadic bursts of internal work that gradually boosted my confidence and diminished my 'give a f**k factor.' It was a process marked by various therapies, strategies, and skills that I learned and applied, each contributing to raising the bar of my confidence bit by bit. However, it wasn't a linear progression upwards; rather, it resembled the jagged edges of a graph, with peaks and valleys over time. There were moments of progress, followed by setbacks, where what I accomplished last week became a hurdle to overcome this week. It often felt like taking two steps forward and one step backward, but through perseverance, I continued to push forward on my journey toward self-assurance.

At first, I believed that simply experiencing everything anew while sober would be enough to bolster my confidence. It seemed like a logical approach, but it quickly became evident that it wasn't the solution. Even after repeating activities multiple times, the discomfort persisted. Whether it was the third, fourth, or tenth time, I still found myself grappling with intense feelings of unease and insecurity. It became clear that my journey towards confidence would require more than just revisiting familiar situations; it would demand a deeper, more nuanced approach to addressing my underlying insecurities and self-image.

In my late 20s, my role shifted from being counselled to becoming more of a counsellor myself. Working in a group home exposed me to many clients' inner thoughts and self-talk, revealing how profoundly their internal dialogue influenced every aspect of their lives. It dawned on me that their inner chatter was shaping their external circumstances. As I observed from the outside, it became clear how crucial self-talk was in determining one's reality. This realization prompted me to turn inward, slow down, and listen closely to my internal dialogue. What I discovered was unsettling – my self-talk was neither kind nor supportive. In fact, it was likely the root cause of many of my problems. I realized that I wouldn't tolerate such negative self-talk from a friend, yet I was subjecting myself to it daily without even realizing it. It became evident that I needed to take control of and change that internal dialogue to move forward.

I devoted myself to consistently challenging those inner voices and transforming how I perceived myself and others. One powerful strategy I employed was the technique of 'acting as if' – essentially, embodying the qualities and characteristics of the person I aspired to become. Each day, I faced challenges by visualizing myself wearing various symbolic "cloaks": sometimes the cape of a superhero, other times the shield of a warrior, and occasionally the cloak of invisibility – each serving a specific purpose for the task at hand. Drawing inspiration from those I admired and respected, I emulated their behaviours and mannerisms, using them as a blueprint for my own transformation. For example, observing how my boss effortlessly worked a room like a seasoned networker, I dissected her approach into actionable strategies that I could adopt. By 'acting as if' I possessed the confidence and social finesse she exhibited, I gradually began to embody those traits and evolve into the person I aspired to be.

The tremors ceased, and a newfound sense of belief in myself began to take root. Moving beyond merely 'acting as if,' I actively sculpted the person I aspired to become, reshaping my self-image by challenging and correcting my negative self-talk. I committed myself to honour my word, recognizing the importance of integrity in building self-respect. Embracing the power of speaking positivity into existence, I carefully chose my words, understanding their impact on my mindset and reality. By deliberately implementing specific strategies, I learned to adapt and evolve, transforming my self-image and confidence in the process. This intentional effort to shape my own narrative has truly changed my life in profound ways.

For instance, I struggled to fully embrace my identity as a photographer. So, one summer, I deliberately chose to carry my photography bag with my tripod visibly hanging on the outside. As I walked around, many people asked, "Are you a photographer?" Initially, my response was hesitant, almost apologetic – a soft "Yes." However, this intentional act of displaying my equipment gradually allowed me to integrate this aspect into my self-image. By the end of the summer, my answer had transformed into an enthusiastic affirmation, as I wholeheartedly embraced this new version of myself.

As part of a promotion, I was faced with the daunting prospect of returning to school for a required diploma. I found myself grappling with intense fear and anxiety. Compounding my apprehension was the fact that the course was located off-campus in an area notorious for violence, ominously dubbed "murder mall" at the time. Despite these daunting circumstances, I made a conscious effort to confront my fears head-on and acknowledge the root of my anxiety. Recognizing that much of my unease stemmed from comparing myself to hypothetical classmates whom I perceived as smarter, younger, and more advanced, I realized the importance of dispelling the unknown. Taking decisive action, I drove out to the location, parked my car, and bravely explored both the mall and the classrooms, reclaiming a sense of familiarity and control over the situation.

On my inaugural day of class, while my nerves were palpable, I found solace in having meticulously addressed as many uncertainties as possible. As I navigated the corridors of the mall enroute to the classroom, an unexpected scene unravelled before me—an altercation that epitomized the very violence I had feared encountering. Reacting swiftly, I brandished my phone, bluffing about capturing the assault and alerting the authorities. The threat alone halted the altercation, sparing my fellow student from harm. Despite lacking an actual camera, the ruse effectively de-escalated the situation. Upon entering the classroom, I made a startling realization—I was the only practitioner in my field amongst my peers, possessing a wealth of experience unmatched by anyone else. By meticulously pre-planning and taking into account all the uncertainties, then shedding the shackles of comparison and confronting challenges head-on, I navigated my first day of school and bolstered my confidence in the process.

I gradually gained the confidence to lead meetings as a manager, deliver presentations to small groups of board members, and stand before gatherings of 200 recovering alcoholics to share my experience, strength, and hope with them. At times, I would have confidently proclaimed that my FOPO had vanished and that I was fully recovered. However, that would only be half the truth.

Through a female running group, I stumbled upon a sense of freedom that would become one of the most precious gifts of my life, shaping my path in ways I could never have imagined. Most of my friends in the group were married, many with grown children or navigating the complexities of empty nests, grandchildren, or aging parents. Each had its own unique journey, distinct from my own. As a gay individual, I had come out during a time when society was hostile towards the LGBTQ+ community, amidst the fear and stigma of the AIDS epidemic. In my adult life, I had grown accustomed to making decisions solely for myself, without the burden of familial expectations or societal norms. Being gay meant facing disapproval from family and encountering derogatory attitudes towards our relationships, often referred to as mere "lovers." Moreover, the prospect of having children seemed like an unattainable dream, as societal prejudices equated being gay with being a pedophile. Despite these constraints, I recognized a sense of freedom within myself that my heterosexual friends could not fully comprehend.

I was driven by a deep desire to share the freedom I had found with my fellow running sisters. I longed for them to experience the same sense of liberation – the freedom to prioritize themselves, to invest in their own well-being without hesitation, to make decisions autonomously, and to live without the weight of guilt, shame and regret. I wanted them to embrace the power of choice, to revel in the countless possibilities that lay before them. It became my mission to lead by example, to show them the path to this newfound sense of empowerment.

"True freedom is the confidence to be yourself in all circumstances." ~Unknown

---

Starting and transitioning into a coaching role has epitomized the concept of empowering women to attain true freedom. However, coaching has proven to be the ultimate test in building confidence. Marketing oneself, embodying one's brand, and speaking in front of a global audience challenge the decades of personal growth and transformation. The prospect of going live or conducting a masterclass would once again trigger the familiar trembling and shaking of nerves. Despite positioning myself as a confidence coach, the truth was that confidence felt waning. I found myself grappling with FOPO yet again.

In a moment of vulnerability and raw honesty, I confided my fears to my own coach. Her response was blunt yet transformative: "Get over yourself," she said, reminding me that my purpose is to serve others. With those words ringing in my ears, I embraced the mantra, "What other people think of me is none of my business." I embarked on a journey to redefine my self-image, envisioning a version of myself that was bold, confident, and free – one driven by a deep desire to serve, help others and make an impact.

Utilizing my extensive background as a counsellor, crisis worker, and police officer, I've guided hundreds of women through transformative journeys. Drawing from these experiences, I developed a program centred on the fundamental principles of Confidence, Communication, and Connections. This amalgamation of professional expertise and personal growth serves as the cornerstone of my confidence programs, giving rise to the birth of the 3C Coach.

Reflecting on my personal and professional journey, it's clear that transformation is not just about inspiration—it's about actionable steps and practical strategies. These tools propelled me forward, allowing me to overcome fears, redefine my self-image and, ultimately, empower others. Now, I'm excited to share six key tips that have been instrumental in my transformation, and I believe they can be equally impactful for you.

1. Meticulously Address Uncertainties: Take proactive steps to identify and mitigate potential uncertainties or challenges in advance. This can involve thorough planning, preparation, and

consideration of various scenarios to minimize surprise and increase confidence in navigating unfamiliar situations.

2. Embrace the "Act as If" Strategy: When facing challenges of striving to embody a new identity, employ the technique of 'acting as if.' Visualize yourself as the person you aspire to become and emulate the behaviours and characteristics. Over time, this practice can help reshape your self-image and boost your confidence.

3. Harness the Power of Language: Be intentional with your words and their impact on your mindset and reality. Choose words that reflect positivity and empowerment and speak them into existence. You can reinforce a strong and confident self-image by affirming your aspirations and goals with conviction.

4. Take Action to Integrate New Identities: To fully embrace a new aspect of yourself, take tangible steps to integrate it into your daily life. Whether it's carrying equipment or engaging in activities related to your newfound identity, immerse yourself in experiences that reinforce this aspect of your self-image. Over time, consistent action can lead to a more authentic and confident sense of self.

5. Challenge Negative Self-Talk: Combatting negative self-talk is crucial in reshaping your self-image and building confidence. Take proactive steps to challenge and correct negative thoughts, replacing them with positive affirmations and empowering beliefs about yourself.

6. Utilize Symbolic Representation: Employ symbolic representations or visual cues and reinforce desired identities or qualities. This could involve carrying items or wearing attire that aligns with the persona you wish to embody. Over time, these symbols can serve as powerful reminders and catalysts for personal transformation.

As we come to the culmination of this chapter, I want to express my deepest gratitude for joining me on this journey of self-discovery and empowerment. I hope that the insights shared and the tips provided have ignited a spark within you, inspiring you to embrace your own path toward confidence and, ultimately, freedom.

As a valued reader, I'm delighted to provide you with exclusive bonus content to enrich your experience further. By purchasing this book, you'll gain complimentary access to the first lesson of my online course, "Scale Your Confidence." This powerful lesson will equip you with practical strategies to cultivate unshakable self-assurance and unlock your full potential.

To claim your bonus and embark on this transformative journey, simply visit https://www.karenscoachingkorner.com/confbookbonus. Let's continue growing together, nurturing the confidence, connections, and sense of purpose that will propel you toward a truly fulfilling life.

Karen Vaile

From the depths of social anxiety and alcoholism, Karen Vaile emerged as a beacon of hope for women seeking true freedom. Her journey is not just a story of personal triumph but a roadmap for those yearning to break free from the shackles of self-doubt and societal expectations.

Karen's two-decade stint as a counsellor, followed by 15 intense years as a 911 police responder, gave her a front-row seat to the human struggle with fear and insecurity. These experiences, coupled with her own battles, forged the foundation of her transformative approach to confidence-building.

Now, as a celebrated coach and #1 International Best-Selling author, Karen ignites a revolution of self-empowerment. She challenges women to shed limiting beliefs, silence their inner critics, and boldly prioritize their own desires. Her mission? To guide women toward a life unburdened by regrets, resentments, or the suffocating weight of others' opinions.

Karen's methods, born from years of introspection and real-world application, offer more than just temporary relief. They provide a sustainable path to unwavering self-assurance. Through her work, Karen doesn't just help women find their voice – she empowers them to use it, unapologetically.

In a world that often dims women's light, Karen Vaile is a testament to the transformative power of confidence, inspiring countless others to illuminate their own paths to freedom.

Connect with Karen at

https://www.karenscoachingkorner.com.

CHAPTER 8

Embrace Your Radiance: Unleashing Confidence in Midlife

Katie Sevenants

To my loving husband, whose unwavering belief in me has been my greatest strength. Your constant support, patience, and calm have allowed me to spread my wings and pursue my dreams. Thank you for being my rock and my inspiration. I am forever grateful for you.

Do you want to have more fun?

Do you want healthy relationships?

Do you want to make a difference in the world?

Picture this: you're standing on top of a mountain, the crisp air hitting your face as you look out over a breathtaking landscape. The sun bathes everything in a golden glow, casting shadows and highlighting the contours of the land below. You feel exhilarated, peaceful, a perfect mix of awe and gratitude for the beauty around you. In front of you lies an endless array of possibilities, each one more exciting than the last. This, my dear reader, is your midlife. Not a time for retreat, but a grand adventure, a thrilling new chapter where you're the star. Buckle up, because we're about to dive into rediscovering your confidence and radiance in midlife!

I've spent over two decades running a successful direct sales beauty business. I'm a certified ELITE Makeup Artist, Color Theory and Skincare Pro Advisor, State Leader, and speaker/trainer in the beauty industry. My passion? Empowering women to discover and embrace their true beauty through both my professional expertise and personal journey. As a wife of 34 years and a mom to three amazing, independent daughters, I get it. I've been where you are, and I'm here to share insights, strategies, and encouragement to help you thrive in this next chapter of life.

More importantly than what I do, is WHY I do it. You see...

I **believe**... When we recognize our own unique talents and abilities, we radiate confidence inside and out.

I **believe**... We can support each other in business and life by being inspired by each other rather than comparing and competing.

I **believe**... We can accomplish so much more and can make a bigger difference in our community when we connect, collaborate, and encourage each other.

I feel extremely blessed. I'm 61 years old and living my best life. I've got a close relationship with my adult daughters, and we make time to get together and celebrate each other often. We even have our own family text chat that we use almost daily just to connect, share jokes, photos, and our daily adventures crossing three states!

I've been running my beauty business from home for 22 years and continue to be in the top 1% of my company. I've earned many company incentives like car lease payments and trips around the world. And the best part is, I've helped thousands of women over the years to feel confident in their own skin.

My husband and I now love to hike, kayak, snowshoe, and play a bit of pickleball (like every other adult on the planet), and I'm excited for the future—looking forward to more travel and adventures in the years to come.

I consider myself lucky to live in Colorado, where I can walk out of my house and hit a trail in just a few minutes.

I've earned many of the top awards in my company, inspired groups of women business owners, and am so thankful to have a business that allows me the freedom to travel and build my business from anywhere I choose.

The Mirror Moment

Not long ago, I stood in front of the mirror, feeling the weight of time. The wrinkles around my eyes seemed deeper, and gray strands had woven themselves into my hair, whispering of wisdom but also hinting at a youth slipping away. As a makeup artist and skincare expert, I spent my days helping women feel beautiful, yet when I looked at myself, I struggled to see beyond the imperfections.

In my 50s, a pivotal decade of change, I found myself at a crossroads. My daughters, once dependent on me, had grown into confident, independent adults. While proud of their accomplishments, I felt a pang of uncertainty—a sense of fading relevance in a world that often prizes youth above all else.

The beauty industry, my professional playground for over two decades, seemed to echo my insecurities. Everywhere I turned, youth was celebrated, and I couldn't help but question my place. Was I tech-savvy enough to keep up with the rapidly evolving digital landscape?

Did I still possess the creativity and passion that fueled my early career successes? These doubts gnawed at me, threatening to overshadow the confidence I once exuded.

At times, the weight of these uncertainties felt suffocating. I considered abandoning my dream—a flourishing business that had afforded me the freedom to travel, nurture my family, and inspire countless women around the globe. The thought of trading it all for a conventional 9-to-5 job left me feeling trapped, my dreams slipping through my fingers like grains of sand.

But deep within me stirred a flicker of resilience—a spark that refused to be extinguished. I sought guidance from mentors who helped me realize that the solution wasn't external; it lay within me. I began investing in myself, shifting my mindset from self-doubt to self-discovery. With each passing day, I embraced my journey, celebrating both my triumphs and failures without fear of judgment.

Slowly but surely, I started to show up authentically—in my business, in my personal life and, most importantly, in front of that mirror. I learned to see beyond the superficial and embrace the beauty that comes with experience and self-acceptance. My wrinkles became badges of honor, each telling a story of resilience and growth. The gray in my hair became a symbol of wisdom earned through years of navigating life's twists and turns.

Today, as I write this, I am proof that transformation is possible at any age. I've walked the path from doubt to empowerment, and I'm here to guide you on your own journey of self-discovery. Together, we'll illuminate the path forward, celebrating your unique beauty and unlocking the limitless potential that lies within.

Embrace Your Unique Beauty

First things first: Let's talk about beauty. Yes, the kind that comes in fancy bottles and compacts, but more importantly, the kind that radiates from within. As someone who's spent over two decades in the beauty industry, I've seen firsthand the transformative power of a little lipstick and mascara. But the real magic? It happens when you embrace the beauty that's uniquely yours.

Let's play a little game. Grab a mirror. No, seriously, do it, put your book down, I'll wait. Now, take a good look. Notice those laugh lines? They're proof of countless moments of joy. The silver streaks in your hair? Badges of wisdom earned through life's ups and downs. Every mark, every line, tells a story—your story. And trust me, It's a bestseller.

Beauty isn't about fitting into a mold or chasing eternal youth. It's about celebrating who you are right now. Try this: Each morning, as you're getting ready, take a moment to compliment yourself. Maybe it's your sparkling eyes, your radiant smile, or even the way your hair catches the light. Make it a habit and watch how this small act transforms your perception of yourself.

Unleash Your Inner Brilliance

Now, let's dive deeper. Beyond the surface lies something even more precious—your inner brilliance. This isn't about what you do, but who you are. Your experiences, your strengths, your quirks—they all add up to a uniquely valuable individual.

I want you to think back to a moment when you felt truly proud of yourself. Was it landing a big project at work? Raising wonderful, independent children? Maybe it was summoning the courage to try something new, like kayaking or learning to play the ukulele. Hold onto that feeling. That's your inner brilliance shining through.

But here's the kicker: We often let self-doubt and imposter syndrome creep in and undermine our worth. It's like having a tiny critic on your shoulder, whispering all the reasons why you're not enough. Time to flick that critic away and embrace your inner cheerleader instead.

Start by jotting down a list of your strengths and accomplishments. Did you raise children? Manage a household? Do you volunteer? Are you an amazing gardener? Big or small, we celebrate them all. Then, whenever doubt starts to creep in, read that list. Remind yourself of your value, because darling, you've got a lot to offer.

Harness Your Potential for Growth

Alright, you're glowing with newfound beauty and basking in your value. What's next? Growth, my friend. This chapter of your life is bursting with potential, and it's time to harness it.

Let's get practical. Think about something you've always wanted to do but never got around to. Maybe it's writing a book, starting a garden, or launching a business. Whatever it is, now's the time. And guess what? You've already got everything you need to make it happen.

During the year of lockdown from Covid, our entire family lived together again under one roof. Two of our girls were home from their colleges, our oldest and her husband moved in when they found out they were pregnant with our first grandchild, and we moved my Mother-In-Law in when her dementia prevented her from living alone. To say it was a full house is an understatement. What I loved about that crazy year of togetherness was realizing how important and short our time together is. So, my husband and I made it a priority to spend Saturday mornings together, just the two of us. We took up hiking...not just a little trail around the neighborhood but hikes into the gorgeous Rocky Mountains of Colorado! While some people were huddled together in their homes, we would escape to the wilderness and push our midlife selves to our limits. We even finished a 14er (that's a mountaintop over 14,000 feet for those of you not from Colorado).

That weekly adventure became our starting point for new midlife adventures. We now enjoy snowshoeing, kayaking, and travel...as often as we possibly can. We have taken cooking classes in most countries we travel to: Spain, Mexico, and most recently Costa Rica. We booked a bike riding tour through Seville, Spain that was about 16 miles in total (yes, my rear was feeling it a few days later) and I hadn't been on a bike in several years. We are living our best life and experiencing new things together!

Set aside a quiet moment and visualize your future self. Imagine five years from now, living your best, most fulfilling life. What are you doing? Who are you spending time with? Most importantly, how do you feel? Putting your feelings to your dreams and goals is the key to manifesting what you want. Now, let's break it down. What's one small step you can take today to move towards that vision? It could be signing up for a class, reaching out to a mentor, making a new friend or even just making a bucket list of goals.

Remember, growth isn't a sprint; it's a journey. Celebrate each milestone, no matter how small. And don't be afraid to step outside your comfort zone. That's where the magic happens.

Overcoming Obstacles

Of course no adventure is without its obstacles. You might hit a few bumps along the way, but guess what? That's perfectly normal. The key is to recognize these challenges and tackle them head-on.

One common hurdle is time. Between work, family, and other commitments, finding time for yourself can feel like a Herculean task. But here's a secret: You don't have to carve out hours each day. Start small. Fifteen minutes of focused effort can make a world of difference. Maybe it's waking up a bit earlier, or perhaps it's using a lunch break to work on your passion project.

I get up 30 minutes earlier to write in my gratitude journal and visualize the emotions and feelings that go along with my ideal future self. Just me, my coffee and my mindset. My tip for visualizing your future life is to see it as if it's already happened. Think about how you are feeling in your future life and who is with you cheering you on.

Another obstacle might be the fear of failure. It's natural to worry about what could go wrong, but here's the thing—every great success story includes a few failures. They're not setbacks; they're steppingstones. Each misstep is an opportunity to learn and grow. Embrace them, and keep moving forward.

Building a Supportive Network

Okay, fabulous friend, let's get one thing straight—no woman is an island. And thank goodness for that, right? The beauty of this stage in life is realizing the power of community. Building a supportive network is crucial. Picture a circle of friends who uplift and inspire you, who cheer for you as loudly as you cheer for them. These are your people. Find them. Cultivate these relationships. They can be friends you've had forever, new connections made through shared interests, or even virtual buddies from online communities.

Think about what lights you up and find your tribe. Maybe it's a local hiking club where you can soak up nature and chat about life, a book group that dives into the stories that make your soul sing, or an online forum for entrepreneurs where you can brainstorm and share successes and setbacks. The key is to surround yourself with like-minded individuals who get you and want to see you thrive.

Remember, collaboration always trumps competition. When we lift each other up, we all rise higher. So, be that beacon of support for others, and you'll find that support reflected back to you in spades. Together, we're unstoppable!

Embracing Adventure and Fun

Alright, let's talk about the F-word: FUN. Yes, fun! This chapter of your life isn't just about ticking off goals and chasing achievements. It's about joy, laughter, and adventure. You've earned it, so let's dive in headfirst.

Think back to a time when you felt truly alive, free from worries and responsibilities. Was it dancing the night away with friends, exploring a new city, or simply laughing until your sides hurt? That's the feeling we're after. Let's bottle that essence and sprinkle it generously throughout our days.

Make a list of activities that bring you joy. Maybe it's something you used to love but haven't done in years, or something entirely new that you're curious about. Is it painting, traveling, trying out a new sport, or learning a musical instrument? Whatever it is, prioritize it. Schedule these joy-bringing activities into your life regularly. Make them non-negotiable. Prioritize fun, and watch how it transforms your outlook.

Your Midlife Makeover in Action

Alright, let's weave all this magic together. Picture yourself waking up each morning, not dreading the day but excited about the possibilities. You start with a few moments of self-appreciation, acknowledging your unique beauty—those laugh lines, those silver strands. You glance at your list of strengths and accomplishments and feel a surge of confidence. With a clear vision of your goals, you take a small but meaningful step forward. Throughout the day, you connect with your supportive network, sharing laughs, insights, and encouragement. And you end the day doing something that makes your heart sing—something purely for the joy of it.

This, my dear, is your Midlife Makeover. It's not about drastic changes or chasing an impossible ideal. It's about embracing who you are, celebrating your journey, and stepping boldly into the future with confidence, joy, and a zest for life.

Write Your Own Story

As we wrap up this chapter, remember that your story is yours to write. You hold the pen, and the possibilities are endless. Age is just a number, and you're in the prime of your life, ready to create the most vibrant, fulfilling chapter yet.

So, go ahead—embrace your radiance, unleash your inner brilliance, and harness your potential. The adventure awaits, and it's going to be amazing. Here's to the best and most fun chapter of your life. Cheers to you, beautiful!

Katie Sevenants

Katie Sevenants is an Inspirational Speaker, Beauty Industry Expert, and Entrepreneur.

With over two decades in the beauty industry, Katie has mastered the art of helping individuals look and feel their best. As a renowned business leader and entrepreneur, she has built a thriving beauty business and is dedicated to empowering midlife women to embrace their confidence and shine in their personal and professional lives.

Katie's mission as an inspirational speaker is to help women break free from self-doubt and comparison, unlocking their unique potential. She encourages clients to find inspiration in others while recognizing their own beauty and individuality. Her approach, rooted in positivity, humor, and spontaneity, transforms personal growth into an enjoyable journey.

Through engaging coaching and community, Katie promotes empowerment, self-acceptance, and self-love, enabling women to confidently pursue their dreams. Her vibrant personality and deep knowledge of beauty, business, and confidence inspire audiences to take actionable steps toward becoming their best selves.

Katie's mission is to celebrate individuality, embrace confidence, and redefine beauty standards for women in their prime. Her motivational speaking style leaves audiences inspired and ready to embark on their own journeys of self-assuredness and fulfillment.

Connect with Katie at www.TheMidlifeMakeover.com.

CHAPTER 9

Beyond the Broken Mirror

Kendra Buffon

To my parents, for your unwavering love. To my husband, my rock and biggest supporter. To my daughter, the shining light that inspires me every day to be the best version of myself. And to anyone battling self-doubt—this is for you. Embrace your strength, reclaim your confidence,
and know you are enough.

"I thought the mirror was my enemy, but it was my lack of confidence that truly held me captive." ~Kendra Buffon

---

Here's the hard truth about confidence – it's not a gift wrapped up with a pretty bow; it's a conquest. It's a choice, a practice, and sometimes, it's a full-on battle. For years, I let self-doubt take the wheel, steering me straight into the abyss of self-destruction. This is the raw, unfiltered story of how my struggle with confidence spiraled into an eating disorder and how reclaiming my self-worth became the most transformative journey of my life. In this chapter, we'll explore the massive impact confidence has on our lives and how choosing it can lead to ultimate freedom.

Early Signs of Lack of Confidence

From the outside, my childhood seemed perfect. Loving parents, a cozy home, a decent school. But underneath it all, there was this constant current of doubt and insecurity. My parents, bless them, tried to protect me from everything, wrapping me in a bubble of overprotection influenced by their strong religious views. Their intentions were golden, but the result? I felt suffocated.

One memory sticks out. Sixth grade. We were supposed to watch a health video about the human body. Permission slips went home, and my mom promptly denied mine. So while my classmates sat in the auditorium, whispering and giggling about puberty and all the changes that come with it, I was the only one left out. I was stuck in a different classroom, feeling the sting of being different.

As a normal human, I was curious about the human body. My own body was changing, and I had questions and feelings I didn't fully understand. But being excluded from that health video made me feel ashamed of my curiosity. I felt guilty for wanting to know more about myself, for having the same questions that my peers were freely exploring. That small incident planted a seed of self-doubt that grew into a forest.

Then came high school. Freshman year was a total disaster. I had a best friend, and we did everything together. You know, like the dynamic duo of awkward teen years. One day, a "popular" girl, who probably took a master class in Mean Girls 101, told me some scandalous gossip about my bestie. Thinking I was playing the hero, I told my friend. But high school politics are savage, y'all. My friend confronted the "popular" girl, who twisted the story and made me the villain. My so-called best friend believed her. Poof! Suddenly, the whole squad turned against me.

Not only did they call me names like ugly and stupid to my face, but they also left cruel comments everywhere, making sure their words were public for everyone to see.

And to top it off, they called me dumb because I spelled "Brazil" as "Brasil." Newsflash: that's how you spell it in Brazil! I was proud of my Brazilian roots, but they turned it into a punchline.

PE class with these girls? Nightmare. I remember hiding in the locker room, crying, and wishing I could teleport to another dimension. I was lost, questioning everything. The mean girls made me doubt myself—what was right, what was wrong, and whether I could trust my own instincts. Freshman year became a daily struggle for my self-esteem, reinforcing the guilt and shame I already felt.

After high school, I was desperately searching for solace, for love, for acceptance. I thought I found it in a long-distance relationship. But instead of the love and acceptance I craved, I found control and manipulation. His constant criticism of my appearance and incessant demands chipped away at my self-esteem. I stayed, even when I found signs of infidelity. Why? Because my sense of self-worth was so low, I didn't believe I deserved better.

At the same time, I entered fashion school, a world where appearance was everything. If my relationship hadn't already demolished my self-esteem, fashion school certainly finished the job. One day, a teacher projected an image of a model on the screen and declared, "This is what you need to look like to succeed in this industry." Those words hit me like a freight train. It was the final blow to my fragile sense of self.

By that point, my life had been a series of events that left me constantly seeking approval and questioning my worth. The relentless pursuit of acceptance and the uncertainty of what was right or wrong had eroded my confidence. I felt completely lost, desperate to control something in my life. And so, I turned to the only thing I felt I could control: food.

The Darkest Times

My eating disorder started innocently enough. A simple, almost harmless desire to lose a few pounds quickly turned into an obsession that took over my life. I restricted myself to no more than 500 calories a day, pushing my body to the brink at the gym. I knew the calorie count of every food item, meticulously tracking every bite. But it was never enough. My self-doubt was a relentless whisper in my ear, convincing me I needed to be thinner, smaller, almost invisible to feel worthy.

Anorexia soon morphed into bulimia, plunging me into an even darker place. The shame of using a toothbrush to make myself vomit is something I'll never forget. Night after night, I was hunched over the sink, tears streaming down my face, gagging and retching, desperately trying to purge every carb, every ounce of guilt and self-hatred that came with each bite of food. My hair began to fall out in clumps, each lost strand a glaring reminder of my crumbling health.

At 5'8", I weighed just 99 pounds. My father's words still haunt me. "What happened to your hair, Kendra?" he asked, concern etched on his face. I hadn't noticed until that moment. I looked in the mirror and saw a ghost staring back. My once-thick blonde locks were now thin and brittle. But it wasn't just me in that reflection—it was Anna, my anorexia, staring back at me with hollow, lifeless eyes. She had stripped away my confidence, leaving behind a frail shadow of who I once was.

Desperate to regain even a shred of my former self, I turned to hair extensions. They became my armor, a way to mask the damage and present a facade of normalcy. I became obsessed, always needing more extensions to cover the ever-thinning strands. Each new addition was a temporary fix for my shattered self-esteem, but it never addressed the deeper issues. My lack of confidence fueled this desperate charade, as I clung to anything that might momentarily make me feel whole, even if it was all an illusion.

You see, it wasn't just about the food or the weight. It was about control, fear, and a deep-seated belief that I wasn't good enough. My lack of confidence drove me to these extremes, making me believe that I needed to be perfect on the outside to feel okay on the inside. But no matter how many extensions I added, how many pounds I lost, it was never enough. The real issue was my shattered confidence, and until I addressed that, nothing would truly change.

Turning Point

The turning point came in the form of an intervention. My family's desperate pleas, especially the sight of my brothers crying, should have hit me like a ton of bricks. But it didn't. Their voices, shaking with fear, told me I was dying. And you know what? I didn't even care. That's how deep I was in my own pit of despair. I had lost all love for myself. I was so far gone that the idea of dying seemed almost... comforting.

Can you imagine? I had sunk to a place where my own destruction seemed like a cozy escape. The girl who once had dreams and plans was now a shell, numb to the world. I had accepted my fate like it was some kind of twisted destiny, and fighting for myself felt as pointless as trying to catch a unicorn.

Then a doctor laid it out for my parents in the starkest terms: "I don't know how she's still alive." That shook them to their core, but for me, it was just another fact. I remained detached, almost indifferent. But my parents, seeing no other way to save me, made the decision to put me into a clinic. Their desperation turned into decisive action, fueled by the hope that maybe, just maybe, this would bring me back to life.

I was sent to a clinic, though the first experience was more traumatizing than healing. It wasn't until I entered a reputable clinic in Arizona that things began to change. This place was different. The staff was compassionate and genuinely cared about my recovery. They helped me peel back the layers of my disorder, revealing the deep-seated issues that fueled it. I started to understand the depth of my disorder and the underlying lack of confidence that had driven me to such extremes. I left the clinic not completely cured, but with a newfound acceptance of my situation. Healing is never a straight line, and part of that journey meant confronting some of the most toxic elements in my life.

The Breaking Point

Remember that toxic ex? Our relationship was a constant rollercoaster, a toxic cycle that seemed impossible to break. Every time I went back to him, it felt like I was undoing all the progress I had made. His manipulative words chipped away at my fragile self-esteem, making me doubt myself all over again. But every time I managed to pull away, I felt a little stronger, a little more sure of my worth.

Then one day, I hit my breaking point. I couldn't take it anymore. Summoning every ounce of strength I had regained, I decided to end it once and for all. I blocked his number, deleted his contacts, and cut off all ties. It wasn't easy—those emotional ties and the fear of being alone were strong—but I knew I had to do it. I had to reclaim my life, my confidence, my sense of self-worth.

But, of course, he found a way to reach out one last time. I remember the day he sent me that particularly nasty email, his words dripping with venom. No need to rehash all the details, the important thing is...

Something inside me snapped. Nope, not today, Satan. I thought. You're not going to let this define you, Kendra. It was like a switch flipped inside me. I wasn't going to let his cruel words undo all the hard work I had put into rebuilding myself. I had come too far, fought too hard, to let him tear me down again.

The Role of Love

A couple of years later, after continuing to heal and grow, I met the love of my life. Enter my now-husband. This man walked into my life and became my rock, my cheerleader, and sometimes, the tough-love coach I desperately needed.

When we first met, he had no idea about the struggles I was still facing. One night, he suggested we order in some Brazilian pizza. If you don't know, Brazilian pizza is next-level—they have the most unexpected, mouthwatering toppings you could imagine. I'm talking everything from Doritos and ribs to chocolate and strawberries. So, there we were, and he orders a pizza with steak and french fries on top. Yes, you heard that right—steak and french fries on a pizza! Sounds bizarre, I know, but trust me, it's a flavor explosion you wouldn't believe.

But as I stared at that pizza, trying to muster the courage to take a bite, my mind raced with panic. "Pizza with french fries on top? Carb on carb? How could I possibly eat this?" Meanwhile, he was blissfully unaware, happily devouring each slice with a big, contented smile. He thought he was being so thoughtful, planning this date night for us. Poor guy, he had no clue I was on the verge of a full-blown meltdown over a slice of pizza.

In those early years together, his unwavering support and tough love became my lifeline. He refused to let me hide behind excuses, pushing me to confront the very fears and insecurities I had been avoiding. His steadfast belief in me ignited a spark, making me realize I was capable of so much more than I ever believed. Slowly but surely, I began to see myself not as a failure but as a survivor. With every challenge I overcame, I started to reclaim my confidence, piece by piece.

Building confidence wasn't just about facing the big, scary fears—it was also about letting go of the small, self-sabotaging habits that kept me from fully embracing who I am and loving myself unconditionally. Little by little, I began to shed the negative behaviors that had defined my life for so long. I stopped counting every calorie, allowed myself to enjoy food without guilt, and started to rebuild my relationship with my body.

A New Beginning: Pregnancy

Just when I thought I was finally nailing this whole self-love thing, life threw me the ultimate curveball: pregnancy. It was like the universe was saying, "Oh, you think you've got this self-acceptance down? Let's see how you handle this!" But instead of freaking out, I felt something completely different—something amazing.

Pregnancy became this incredible beacon of hope and proof of my body's resilience. It wasn't just about me anymore; it was about this tiny heartbeat inside of me. That realization sparked a fierce, protective love I didn't even know I had. As my body grew and changed, I was in awe of its power and adaptability. My focus shifted from obsessing over being thin to cherishing the life I was growing.

This journey wasn't just about my physical transformation; it was a total shift in my mindset and spirit. Every stretch mark, every extra pound became a badge of honor, a symbol of my body's miraculous ability to create life. Pregnancy shattered the chains of my eating disorder, teaching me to celebrate my body for its strength and capability, not just for how it looked.

Pregnancy wasn't just an experience; it was a rebirth for me too. It kicked off a new chapter where I embraced my body with gratitude and love. This was my beautiful transformation. This was my new beginning.

A Symbolic Shedding: Hair Extensions

There's one moment in my journey that will forever stand out. It was my daughter's second birthday. After years of depending on hair extensions, they fell out. Just like that. Poof. Gone. It had never happened before, but on that significant day, they did.

I stood there, stunned and vulnerable, staring at my reflection. And then it hit me—there she was: the real me. In that instant, the last remnants of my self-doubt and lack of confidence fell away with those extensions. It was a powerful, symbolic shedding of all my past insecurities. My natural hair, growing back stronger and healthier, was a reflection of my internal transformation. But let's be real—it wasn't about the hair. It was about fully embracing myself, in all my raw, unfiltered glory. I realized my worth had nothing to do with my appearance. My confidence was forged deep within, anchored in the truth that I was enough, exactly as I am.

My daughter? She was the cherry on top, the perfect end to my journey. She reflected the strength and resilience I'd found within myself. But let's be clear—my journey to recovery and confidence wasn't some magical fairy tale. It was built on the choices I made every single day. I chose to ditch toxic habits. I chose to see my worth. I chose to fight for my health and happiness. My daughter didn't save me; she highlighted the beauty of the life I fought so hard to build.

Life After Recovery

Overcoming my eating disorder didn't just change my life—it transformed it. I learned to prioritize my well-being and set healthy boundaries. I surrounded myself with positive influences and began to rebuild my self-esteem. Those past struggles didn't just challenge me—they forged me into an unbreakable force of strength and resilience. Today, I stand tall as a confident mother, wife, friend, and daughter, living a life overflowing with self-love and acceptance.

And let me tell you, I can now sit down and savor that infamous pizza with french fries on top. Yes, that same combo that once threw me into a full-blown panic attack is now one of my absolute favorites. No guilt, no fear—just pure, cheesy delicious joy.

Recovery and Confidence

Recovery and confidence are deeply intertwined. Healing my body was just the start; healing my mind was where the real magic happened. Confidence isn't something that just shows up at your door; it's built through action. It's about facing your fears head-on and proving to yourself that you can conquer them. Every single guilt-free meal and every moment I looked in the mirror and saw my true self—not a ghost of my former life—was a victory in reclaiming my confidence.

Recovery demanded that I confront those nasty, negative beliefs head-on and replace them with affirmations of worthiness. It required digging deep, forgiving myself for years of harm, and learning to love myself fiercely. Confidence emerged from recognizing my inner strength and the daily courage to battle my demons. It's about standing tall, embracing your true self, flaws and all, and declaring, "This is me, and I am enough." Each setback taught me, and each triumph fortified me. Confidence isn't about never failing; it's about knowing you're strong enough to rise every single time you fall.

Choosing Confidence

Choosing confidence is no easy task; it's a bold, life-altering decision that demands courage and commitment. It means waking up every single day and boldly declaring that you are deserving of love, happiness, and success. By sharing my journey, I hope to ignite a spark within you, inspiring you to take that crucial first step toward healing and self-acceptance.

Remember, this transformation isn't instant. It requires time, relentless perseverance, and an unshakable belief in your own worth. You will face setbacks, and there will be moments of doubt. But each day you choose to believe in yourself, you grow stronger and more resilient. Never, ever give up on yourself. You are worth every bit of the fight, every moment of the journey, and every step toward becoming the incredible person you are meant to be. Believe in your power, your strength, and your worth, because you are capable of extraordinary things.

Kendra Buffon

Kendra Buffon is a passionate content director and author, dedicated to helping you crush self-doubt and unlock your true potential. Leading a team of exceptional professionals, she crafts compelling stories and strategies that elevate businesses online.

In her chapter, Beyond the Broken Mirror, Kendra shares her inspiring journey of overcoming self-doubt and an eating disorder, offering practical insights and hope for anyone ready to reclaim their self-worth.

As a fierce advocate for mental health and self-love, Kendra inspires young adults, parents, and anyone who's ever felt less than. Her authentic voice has established her as an emerging thought leader, aspiring to deliver impactful presentations and engage in various speaking engagements to empower others.

Kendra believes in breaking free from societal pressures and redefining success on one's own terms. For her, true fulfillment comes from inner peace, self-acceptance, and celebrating your true self. Beyond her professional accomplishments, she finds her deepest fulfillment in motherhood, guiding her daughter to grow into a confident and empowered woman.

And yes, she loves a good glass of Sangria.

Connect with Kendra at www.kendrabuffon.com.

CHAPTER 10

Do It BECAUSE You're Scared!

Lynda Sunshine West

This chapter is dedicated to anyone who has ever allowed a fear to stop them from doing something they truly wanted to do and has regretted it.

When I was five years old, I ran away from home and was gone an entire week. I only went to the next-door neighbor's house, but for me it felt like I was gone forever. I'm sure the neighbor called my mom and told her I was there, but Mom let me stay. I expected my parents to come and get me after a day, but one day turned into seven before my mom called the neighbor and said, "Lynda's been gone long enough. You can send her home now."

I believe my mom was trying to teach me a lesson, but that week became instrumental in shaping my belief system. No one came to get me, and I developed a firm belief that no one wanted me around and nobody loved me. At five years old, this belief was locked in tight and stayed with me for the next 46 years until I was 51 years old.

When I came home, I did so with my tail between my legs and my head bent down, literally. Growing up in an abusive home, I was afraid to look my parents in the eyes, and that fear extended to others for many years. I was riddled with fear and became a people-pleaser as a result. Whenever people asked me to do anything, I would say "YES" because I was afraid they wouldn't like me if I said "NO."

High school was a petri dish for fear. While I was saying yes to my friends, I was also lashing out at other students. If I could turn back time, I would never have made fun of that girl with Down syndrome. If I could remember her name, I would fall to my knees and beg for her forgiveness. My efforts to please one group caused me to be mean to others. Even my friends made fun of me, so I started making fun of myself. The mean girl became mean to herself. I became my own worst enemy.

This behavior of being mean to myself and allowing others to be mean to me didn't get any better after high school. Right out of high school, I married someone just like my dad. I didn't recognize it as an abusive relationship because it was just a continuation of how I had grown up. My first husband yelled at me daily, saying, "You're so stupid. You're so ignorant. People are only nice to you because they feel sorry for you." And, unfortunately, I believed him and adopted his beliefs about me to be my own.

I ended the marriage after two years and two babies.

It's incredible what emotional and mental damage can happen in just two short (what felt like eternity) years. I decided one day that I wasn't going to stay in an abusive relationship like my mom did, so I walked out the door with a diaper bag over one shoulder, my purse over the other, one child on my hip, and one child in her baby carrying case. That may sound brave, but I did it because my fear of staying was stronger than my fear of leaving.

Sometimes we are faced with two fears and we choose which fear we will allow to stop us and hold us back or which fear will fuel us forward. I took my fear of staying in that abusive relationship as fuel to tap into my five-year-old little girl bravery and "run away" again.

My professional life had its own set of issues. I moved from job to job to job: fast food worker, 4H poop scooper, bank teller, data entry clerk at Fortune 500 companies, legal secretary for a judge in the Ninth Circuit Court of Appeals. Any of them could have been a long-term career, but I usually left within one week to 18 months of being hired. In many cases, I was underappreciated. I came up with new ideas, and no one would listen. I frequently heard phrases like, "But we've always done it this way." I was afraid of saying the wrong thing and people thinking I was stupid and whenever I did something "right," people called me a brown-noser. I felt like I was stuck between a rock and a hard place.

So, I started to shut down. I stopped using my voice.

Was it because I was stupid like my ex-husband said I was?

Were people really only being nice to me because they felt sorry for me?

Could he have been right all along?

I was caught in this cycle where I felt afraid of failing, but I also felt afraid of succeeding. I couldn't find satisfaction in any of my 49 jobs.

In August of 2014, I was driving to work for the judge in the Ninth Circuit Court of Appeals (my 49th job after 36 years) sitting in traffic like I had been doing for several decades. An overwhelming sense of dread, disgust, and anger engulfed my body.

There I was, 51 years old, pounding on the steering wheel and asking, "What is this all about? What is this planet all about? Why are we here? Why do we have to do this? What is my life all about? Literally, WHY AM I HERE? I have no value. I have no purpose. I have no reason to be here."

That day when I got to work, there was a post in a Facebook group that said, "I'm a life coach. I took some time off. I'm getting back into it and am looking for five women who want to change their life." I didn't know what a life coach was, but I knew one thing: she was talking to me. I wanted to change my life. I sent her a private message, said I wanted to work with her, and we worked together for the next four months.

The most instrumental exercise we did together helped me see myself through the eyes of others (positive people only), which, in turn, helped me transform from my own worst enemy into my own best cheerleader.

"See yourself through the eyes of others, for others see the real you." ~Lynda Sunshine West

---

The amount of change that happened during that four-month period of time was astronomical. People were saying to me on a weekly basis, "You're so different this week than you were last week."

When December rolled around, I was on my own, all alone, no more life coach. I had the tools she had given me to keep growing, but I knew deep down that there was a LOT more growth to come. And, just like Veruca Salt in the original Willy Wonka movie, "I wanted it NOW!"

At the end of December, I realized I had become accustomed to changing and growing that I was addicted to the positivity in my life. However, that positivity slowed down because my life coach was no longer with me.

New Year's Eve isn't a big deal for me. My husband and I go to bed early and skip all the festivities. However, when I woke up on January 1, 2015, something was different. I realized I had so many fears that were stopping me from living my life. Rather than setting New Year's Resolutions (because I break them every time), I made a New Year's Commitment: to break through one fear every day that year.

"Every morning for 365 days when I wake up, before getting out of bed, I will ask myself one simple question, three simple words. Then I will wait for the answer to come. The question is, 'What scares me?'" I had no idea how much those three words would change the trajectory of my life. I was in for a wild and crazy ride.

The first three months I faced fears such as talking to strangers, starting a conversation, and going to networking events. I was feeling cautiously optimistic, but fear was still prominent. About three months into facing one fear every day, I was brushing my teeth and reciting an acronym I had heard many times in my life: False Evidence Appearing Real. FALSE EVIDENCE APPEARING REAL. **FALSE EVIDENCE APPEARING REAL**? Staring at myself, I realized that acronym is a lie.

I broke it down and realized that there was nothing false about my fear. My fears are as real as can be to me. There was no evidence in anything. It didn't appear real; it was real. I looked over the previous three months and had this epiphany that when I tapped into my faith, it was much easier for me to break through my fear. You can't have faith and fear at the same time. They are opposites. I also realized that fear is nothing more than anxiety or nervousness, so I came up with my own acronym: Faith Erases Anxious Reactions. When your fear is strong, your faith is weak. That means that when your faith is strong, your fear is weak. You just need to tap into your faith: faith in yourself, faith in others, and faith in God.

Faith Erases Anxious Reactions
~Lynda Sunshine West

I continued the process. Wake up, ask the question, wait for the answer, face the fear THAT DAY.

Over the next 90 days, I conquered fears such as asking someone to do something for me, speaking on stage, and asking a celebrity to endorse my book. After 180 days of facing fears, I looked back on the previous six months and asked myself a question, "What's the common theme between these fears? There's gotta be something." That's when I had another epiphany: the majority of my fears were caused by one overarching fear: the fear of judgment.

Something as simple as starting a conversation with a stranger can be difficult for many of us. In my case, it was the fear of saying something stupid or ignorant and them "catching on to how stupid I am." For others, it may be due to their speaking with an accent or not being an expert on a certain topic. Armed with this knowledge, I was able to tackle the next six months with a mission to rid myself of the fear of judgment. By the end of the year, judgment was no longer an issue for me. I did it.

While I was ridding myself of the fear of judgment, I came up with a simple 7-step process to help me quickly and easily break through fear EVERY TIME and I'm going to share it with you here in hopes that it helps you break through a fear or two to transform your life.

STEP 1 to Break Through Fear

The first thing you need to do is identify a fear you want to over-come. Maybe you're a rockstar at work, but you know you're un-derpaid and are afraid of asking for a raise. Maybe you have a great idea or passion to start a new business, but the idea of starting it paralyzes you. Maybe you're comfortable around friends, but meet-ing new people scares you. Maybe you're comfortable speaking to small groups of people you know, but the idea of getting on stage in front of strangers scares you. I have experienced ALL of these in the past, and, yes, they're all connected to the fear of judgment.

Got your fear in mind? Awesome. Let's go!

To demonstrate my simple 7-step process, let's use speaking on stage as the fear we're going to tackle today. This was actually my greatest fear, the one where my knees were shaking, my throat locked up, my palms were sweaty, and my memory escaped me once I got on stage. (They say more people are scared of speaking on stage than they are of dying. That is false. The truth is that more people are scared of the judgment they 'might' receive while speaking on stage than they are of dying.)

The first question you ask yourself is:

"If I speak on stage right now, will it adversely affect my life <u>one year</u> from today?"

Let's examine this sentence. The first component is to clearly state your fear. Then we come to the phrase "right now." What's happening by asking this question is you are starting to move your brain into a state of logic and moving yourself out of an emotional state of mind.

You see, fear starts in the part of the brain called the amygdala. According to Smithsonian Magazine, "A threat stimulus, such as the sight of a predator, triggers a fear response in the amygdala, which activates areas involved in preparation for motor functions involved in fight or flight." That feeling of fighting or having to run away is a very visceral, emotional reaction that we can feel in our body. What we need to do to overcome fear is to start thinking logically.

Then we add the word "Adversely." Why that word? If you leave out the word "adversely," you're left with "will it affect my life?" Yes, it can affect your life in a positive or a negative way. By adding the word "adversely," you're asking if doing this action will affect your life in a bad way.

Then we have the words "One year." I start here because the majority of fears will not adversely affect your life one year from today. In the case of speaking on stage, the worst thing that may happen is you forget part of your talk and the audience is confused about the point you were trying to make. But a year from now, you may not even remember that day occurred. Time has a way of putting things into

117

perspective. Seeing a situation with this timeframe puts you into a realistic state of mind and that is necessary in order to quickly and easily break through fears.

Finally, we have the words "from today." I was breaking through one fear every single day for a year, so it was important that I break through that fear that day. Waiting until tomorrow meant I would have two fears to break through. This ended up being a brilliant idea because it forced me to exercise my fear-breaking muscle. Breaking through fears became easier and easier because fear became part of my comfort zone. This exercise ENLARGED the size of my comfort zone.

STEP 2 to Break Through Fear

The second step is asking the same full question, but this time changing only the timeframe. "If I speak on stage right now and I mess up, will it adversely affect my life six months from today?" Like the one-year timeframe, there is still no downside.

STEP 3 to Break Through Fear

"If I speak on stage right now and I mess up, will it adversely affect my life one month from today?" Again, no downside, but we are getting closer to the present.

STEP 4 to Break Through Fear

"If I speak on stage right now and I mess up, will it adversely affect my life one week from today?"

Here's where it gets a little funky. Depending on the fear you're facing, one week from breaking through the fear you may still feel a little queasy inside or weird. You may still feel the effects of breaking through that fear. This is because you've moved back into an emotional state of mind, even though, logically, you know you're okay. Let's say, for all intents and purposes, you responded that speaking on stage right now will NOT adversely affect your life one week from today.

As you might have guessed, the next steps are to shorten the timeframe.

STEP 5 to Break Through Fear

"If I speak on stage right now and I mess up, will it adversely affect my life one day from today?"

Let's go for even shorter.

STEP 6 to Break Through Fear

"If I speak on stage right now and I mess up, will it adversely affect my life one hour from today?"

And FINALLY....

STEP 7 to Break Through Fear

"If I speak on stage right now and I mess up, will it adversely affect my life RIGHT NOW?"

You might be wondering why I use seven steps instead of just one. Well, I found that by slowly stepping myself down through each time period, it moved me into a more relaxed state of mind and my logical brain had time to process what I was doing. I was able to more logically answer the questions and not allow my emotions to take over logic and reality.

But what if the answer to the question is YES?

What I have found is that after you break through a fear RIGHT NOW, you rarely have long-term adverse effects. In those cases where an adverse outcome is "possible," you need to come up with a plan of how to address it. You don't just give up and walk away; you simply recognize that additional work needs to be done to overcome that fear.

If you're afraid of asking for a raise, your plan may be to rehearse what you are going to say to your boss and have an outline of WHY you deserve the raise. If you're afraid of starting a new business, you may find a mentor who is successfully doing what you want to do and have them guide you so you gain confidence in starting your business. If you're afraid of speaking on stage, you may rehearse your talk before getting on the stage. If you're afraid of meeting new people, your plan may be to psyche yourself up before talking to them.

I use a word that moves me into a state of confidence and laughter, which also calms my nerves. My word is "SHAZAM!!" What will be your word?

I may not have the same fears as you, but know this, your fears are very real to you and that's what matters.

Decide right here, right now, not to allow anyone to rob you of your experience of that fear by telling you it's insignificant or ridiculous. YOU have the power to break through that fear in the moment, but only you can make that decision. And it has to be a decision that you made FOR YOU.

Yes, fear is scary. But it doesn't have to control your life. In fact, it can make your life better. So when you've identified a fear in your life, face it head-on and Do It BECAUSE You're Scared.

When I wrote my #1 international bestselling book, _Do It BECAUSE You're Scared_, I had fear about writing it. But I didn't let my fear stop me from putting the words onto paper and putting the book into the world where it would either fail or succeed. You see, life isn't about always being right or having the right answers.

Life is a series of "I tried and failed or I tried and succeeded. In both instances, I won because 'I tried.'"
~Lynda Sunshine West

I did it BECAUSE I was scared. Will you?

Lynda Sunshine West

Lynda Sunshine West is the Founder and CEO of Action Takers Publishing and is best known as the Celebrity Bestseller Book Publishing Expert. As a 38-times #1 International Bestselling Author, Speaker, Contributing Writer at Brainz Magazine, Executive Film Producer, and Red Carpet Interviewer, she is dedicated to empowering 5 million women and men to share their.

Lynda's journey began at five years old when she ran away from home and stayed away for an entire week. This early experience left her riddled with fears and turned her into a people-pleaser. By age 51, she decided to break through one fear every day for an entire year. This transformative journey helped her gain immense confidence, which she now uses to help others share their voices.

Growing up in a volatile, abusive alcoholic household and marrying someone just like her father, Lynda's voice was stifled for too long. She felt suppressed, ignored, and judged, leading her to shut down. At 51, she realized fear was stopping her from living, so she decided to break through one fear every day for a year during which she became encouraged to share her voice.

Today, Lynda Sunshine speaks on stages, interviews stars on the red carpet, makes TV and podcast appearances, publishes books, and creates positive and uplifting communities for her clients. She believes in cooperation and collaboration and loves connecting with like-minded people.

Lynda Sunshine helps people get their stories off of their vision board and into the world to make a greater impact on the planet.

Connect with Lynda Sunshine at

https://www.actiontakerspublishing.com.

CHAPTER 11

Blind Confidence™ Have You Outgrown Your Mindset?

Mindy Nelson, MBA, FACHE

In this revolutionary chapter, I challenge you to recognize that your current mindset could be like an outdated pair of glasses—the prescription has not been updated recently, the frames are slightly bent, look like they are from the '80s, and perhaps the lenses are scratched because they have been mishandled. That's ok. All things like glasses wear out. Did you know that your mindset might be old, outdated and maybe you've even outgrown it? You have been viewing the world and, more importantly, yourself through distorted glasses that no longer serve you. It is time for an upgrade. It's time for an update. Let me be the first to welcome you to Blind Confidence.

What's Blind Confidence?

Blind Confidence is about updating, upgrading, and upskilling your mindset. Your old you might not be as effective anymore. Your mindset might not help you rise to the next level of your career or your relationships.

Blind Confidence is not about recklessness or disregard for consequences; it is about trusting your innate ability to navigate life's challenges, even when the path ahead is uncertain. As someone who has walked through adversity personally and professionally, I have learned that Blind Confidence is not just a concept but a necessity. Just like we update our computers, apps and software, just like we update our wardrobe, just like we upgrade our lives as we achieve more, we must also update and upgrade our mindset.

Blind Confidence Can Be a Lesson in Love and Devotion

Let me share a moment that crystallized the essence of Blind Confidence. I am an early riser and was awake before everyone else during a family vacation. The house was silent, and I decided to go for my daily walk on the beach. It was still misty outside and the sleepy beach town where we were staying was just that... sleepy.

As I started my walk to the shoreline, my feet first touched the soft sand and, with each step, my feet sank into the cool, soft sand. The sand got firmer as I approached the shoreline to begin my walk. Soon, I was walking side by side on the shore. I headed north, as I always did. This time, rather than other walkers or joggers in my line of sight, there was a static, unmoving figure ahead. I looked closer as I approached. I could tell it was a man and his dog staring off into the ocean together. I normally would have allowed my eyes to drift in another direction. Instead, though, I looked closer because the dog was not off its leash ready to catch a ball or run into the ocean. This dog was different. This dog lay almost motionless on a makeshift wagon. The wagon had big wheels and knobs on the wheels so that the dog's owner could pull it on the sand. As I approached the owner and the dog, the owner was feeding the dog with one hand and stroking its back with his other hand.

As I continued to walk closer, first 20 feet ahead, then 10 feet ahead, then 5 feet ahead, I could see tears in the owner's eyes. This dog had been his best friend for years. It was likely in its final weeks, if not days. It was thin, frail, and weak but happy.

They were enjoying a peaceful moment—a moment that in times past had been full of much more energy. This time, though, they enjoyed each other's company for what it was. Accepting that times had been good, they knew that this was a new time in their relationship. This was a time that both were facing with courage.

This scene serves as a powerful metaphor for Blind Confidence in our own lives. Like the owner with his aging dog, we often face insurmountable situations. Challenges that we are facing like saying goodbye to a trusted companion, or saying goodbye to a time in our life as we prepare for a new experience ahead. In the moment, emotions and experiences shape our perception of what lies ahead. Sometimes the fear of the unknown causes fear. Sometimes it causes apprehension or anxiety. What we fear is the unknown. Sometimes sitting idle seems more comfortable than taking a step in a new direction. The new direction could be a new job, a new relationship or changes to the people or circumstances with which we are already familiar.

Blind Confidence offers you the encouragement you need to take that next step. Whether it's living moment by moment in what feels uncomfortable or taking a step into the unknown. Regardless, Blind Confidence offers all of us the ability to take a leap of faith, knowing that we can live a more enjoyable, freeing and fulfilling life. Upgrade your thoughts and consider using the concept of Blind Confidence as your copilot to face the unknown.

Blind Confidence Sees Vulnerability as a Strength

Embracing Blind Confidence requires vulnerability—a concept beautifully explored by Brené Brown, research professor and author.

"Vulnerability is not winning or losing; it is having the courage to show up and be seen when we have no control over the outcome." ~Brené Brown

My journey has been a testament to this truth. Each time I have chosen to be vulnerable—whether in leaving an abusive relationship or pursuing single motherhood—I have tapped into a wellspring of strength I did not know I possessed.

Blind Confidence Is Action-Minded

Blind Confidence is about taking that first step, even when your knees are shaking and your palms are sweaty.

"If you have the instinct to act on a goal, you must physically move within 5 seconds, or your brain will kill it."
~Mel Robbins

Blind Confidence is not simply about being fearless but acknowledging your fear and moving forward. This is where REAL growth happens.

Furthermore, bestselling author and podcaster Tim Ferriss echoes this sentiment:

"The most important thing you can do is to do something."
~Tim Ferriss

Take action. Decide and move forward even without 100% of the details.

Blind Confidence Shifts Perspectives

In *Radical Acceptance: Embracing Your Life With the Heart of a Buddha*, psychologist, and meditation teacher Tara Brach offers valuable insight into shifting our perspective to embrace Blind Confidence. She encourages us to practice "radical acceptance"—fully accepting our present situation as a precursor to change. This does not mean resignation; it means acknowledging where we are to see where we want to go.

Blind Confidence Expands Our Choices

Blind Confidence is ultimately about choice. It is choosing to live rather than merely exist. In *The Power of Now: A Guide to Spiritual Enlightenment*, spiritual teacher and author Eckhart Tolle reminds us,

---

"The primary cause of unhappiness is never the situation but your thoughts about it." ~Eckhart Tolle

---

When we choose Blind Confidence, we believe in our capacity to handle whatever comes our way.

Blind Confidence Changes Lives

One of the most profound examples of Blind Confidence in my life was my decision to become a single mother through in vitro fertilization (IVF). This choice required an enormous leap of faith in my abilities, resources, and capacity to love. The process was grueling, filled with medical procedures, emotional rollercoasters, and substantial financial commitments. Like others struggling to become parents, your patience is tested as you navigate the unchartered IVF territory. This process confirmed my suspicion that courage precedes confidence (Smith, 2022).

As a woman who had chased her career across the country and the globe, I collected miles, free nights at hotels, and ate more chicken dinners on airplanes than I can count (yes, these were the days when a meal was more than pretzels or a Biscoff cookie). I also purchased my first house, collected many friends, and even a few pivotal relationships. While I will be forever grateful for those who crossed my path and the career advancements and opportunities to challenge myself and my capabilities and achieve graduate degrees, certifications, and Fellowships, something was still missing. I listened to the nudge until it got so loud that I had no choice but to take action. I did not know the outcome; I took a step of faith or acted with Blind Confidence. What made this decision even more unusual was that I was single. Yes, I am single. I had no partner; however, I had friends and family who supported me from the early stages of my journey.

After a couple of years of exploring my options and undergoing necessary treatments, I was able to meet my daughter. Just like all babies, she was born with her eyes closed. Looking back now, she entered this world on faith and lived on faith that she would meet all her needs long after her eyes opened and began to speak. Now that she is a kid, I still see her child-like faith in trying new things, sometimes eagerly, sometimes with hesitancy; regardless, she tries them, and most of the time, she is always better because of it.

Upon reflection, Blind Confidence was my guiding light through it all. I acted in the moment, lived in the moment, and did my best to put one foot in front of the other. I did not drop all the different things in my life. I was single, after all, and needed my job for income. However, I might not have known that a gentle force, a gentle nudge, was there at the time. I trusted it and moved forward.

It is important to note that this story of chasing the unknown is not just for mothers or aspiring mothers. The essence of Blind Confidence applies to any significant life decision, whether changing careers, starting a business, beginning a new relationship, a new job, or even pursuing a passion project. You do not need to be an expert or know all the statistics to understand the power of leaping into the unknown and chasing something that will improve your life.

Blind Confidence Navigates You Through Turbulent Times

As a trained Cessna pilot, I have learned valuable lessons about Blind Confidence that apply far beyond the cockpit. One crucial aspect of pilot training is instrument flying. Imagine sitting in a simulator with the entire windshield blacked out—much like driving a car with the sunshade completely covering your view. Crazy, I know.

Pilots must rely entirely on their instrument panel to navigate the airplane in these conditions. This simulates flying through clouds or at night with minimal or no visibility of what is around the plane or how high or low the aircraft is flying. In other words, when pilots receive their instrument rating certification, they know how to fly blind. Instrument rating knowledge teaches pilots how to fly planes, especially when the air has turbulence and storms are looming above, below, or ahead. Flying blind as a pilot is not only an excellent skill, but it is also a must-have.

This scenario perfectly encapsulates the essence of Blind Confidence. When you cannot see what is ahead, you must trust your instruments, training, and ability to interpret the information available. You are flying blind, yet you must maintain the confidence to make decisions and adjust your course. We often face situations where our "windshield" is obscured. We cannot see the future clearly, and the future seems uncertain. This is where Blind Confidence comes into play. Like a pilot relying on instruments, we must trust our skills, preparation, and ability to adapt to changing circumstances. Just as a pilot would not take off without proper training and preparation, Blind Confidence does not mean reckless action. It means doing the groundwork, developing your skills, and then having the courage to "take off" even when you cannot see the entire journey ahead. Remember the pilot's mindset, whether you are making a career change, starting a new relationship, or facing any significant life transition. Trust your "instruments"—instincts, experiences, and support systems. Have confidence in your ability to navigate through the fog of uncertainty.

Blind Confidence: Your Updated, Your Upgraded Pair of Glasses

Some might refer to Blind Confidence as a power source. Tap into Blind Confidence every time you need to just like you might tap into your religious and spiritual practices. Blind Confidence is a way of life. It's your updated pair of glasses that helps you see your life, your circumstances and your choices so much more clearly. Blind Confidence empowers you to take action. Choose a new way you want to live. Choose to upgrade your life and soon you will see that on a regular basis your choices will expand, your confidence will grow exponentially and so will your happiness.

Blind Confidence is a way of life.
It's your updated pair of glasses that helps
you see your life.
Your circumstances and your choices so
much more clearer.
~Mindy Nelson

Blind Confidence Can Be Summoned

As your confidence increases, so will your influence as a leader (Neck, 2023). Leaders can be defined as those where you work, family leaders, or friend group leaders. Model the behavior of Blind Confidence.

1. **Embrace Imperfection**: Recognize that perfection is an illusion. As Elizabeth Gilbert, author of *Eat, Pray, Love*, says, "Done is better than perfect" (Gilbert, 2015).

2. **Practice Self-Compassion**: Be kind to yourself. Kristin Neff, pioneer in self-compassion research, teaches that self-compassion is more motivating than self-criticism (Neff, 2011).

3. **Take Micro-Actions**: Start small. James Clear, author of *Atomic Habits*, advocates for the power of tiny changes to create remarkable results (Clear, 2018).

4. **Cultivate Gratitude**: Focus on what you have rather than your lack. This shift in perspective can fuel your confidence.

5. **Surround Yourself with Support**: Build a network of people who believe in you, even when you struggle to believe in yourself.

Blind Confidence Takes Action

Throughout this chapter, we have examined various aspects of Blind Confidence, from the courage to take action in uncertainty to the vulnerability required to show up authentically to the power of shifting our perspectives. We have seen how Blind Confidence can guide us through personal struggles, career decisions, and even in the cockpit of an airplane.

In my years of speaking engagements and mentoring sessions, I have shared these insights with diverse audiences, from corporate executives to aspiring entrepreneurs. Time and again, I have witnessed the transformative power of Blind Confidence in action with individuals, their work teams, and their families.

*Blind Confidence is about being brave
and taking action
even when we don't have all the answers.*
~Mindy Nelson

When we take action, our choices expand, our lives improve, and our relationships grow. We are one step closer to living the life we truly deserve.

Furthermore, Blind Confidence is not just about individual achievement; it's about inspiring others by how we live our lives with confidence. This methodology of thinking, behaving, and acting can be contagious. When we live our lives this way, others around us see it, hear it, and feel it. Blind Confidence is contagious. When we improve, so do the lives of those around us. Blind Confidence is a mutually-benefitting way of living. If you don't start living with Blind Confidence now, then when?

Dedication: Blind Confidence Is a Multi-Generational Gift

As we conclude our exploration of Blind Confidence, I honor my mother's memory and dedicate this chapter to my daughter.

My mom was a woman of courage, strong will, and perseverance. Though her life was mostly good, she faced unexpected adversities yet never gave up. Growing up with a woman who was small in stature but big in courage, I learned to run, not walk, towards what I wanted. As a flight attendant, teacher, and later financial executive, she faced obstacles like mental health crises, economic hardships, and, at the end of her life, unimaginable physical limitations. However, she persevered through it all without complaint, never feeling sorry for herself and giving back more than she received.

Her legacy is one of resilience, hope, and unwavering belief in perseverance. My mom, dad, and bonus dad taught me that no matter the circumstances, we always have the choice to keep going, believe in ourselves, and strive for something better. This is the essence of Blind Confidence—the courage to keep moving forward, even when the path is unclear. It's about trusting your ability to handle whatever comes your way and believing that your efforts will lead to growth and progress, even if the outcome isn't immediately visible.

I further dedicate this chapter to my daughter, whose birth showed me that living blindly with confidence is the only way to live. Although my mom didn't use the term "Blind Confidence," looking back, I see that's precisely what she embodied and passed on to me. My daughter now carries this legacy forward.

My mom believed she could do anything and never hesitated to tell me I could be whoever I wanted. Her life embodied Blind Confidence. She persevered even to the last day of her life. She taught me that no matter the circumstances, we always have the choice to keep going, believe in ourselves, and strive for something better.

My daughter's birth reinforced this belief, showing me that living with Blind Confidence is not just an ideal but a necessity. Her presence in my life reminds me daily of the power of unwavering belief and the courage to pursue our dreams, no matter the obstacles.

Blind Confidence and Self-Reflection

Blind Confidence is about living purposefully and creating a ripple effect that touches everyone we encounter. In my work with C-suite executives and VPs, I've seen how this mindset can revolutionize leadership and organizational culture. It fosters an environment where innovation thrives because people feel empowered to take calculated risks.

Moreover, as you move forward from here, I encourage you to reflect on your journey. Where have you demonstrated Blind Confidence without realizing it? How can you cultivate more of it in your life? Remember, embracing Blind Confidence does not mean you will always succeed, but you will always be moving forward, learning, and growing.

The time to live with Blind Confidence is now. Your life is a precious gift. Please do not watch it pass you by. Embrace Blind Confidence, shift your perspective, elevate your thinking, and activate your options. The world is waiting for the unique contribution that only you can make.

Blind Confidence: Join the Movement

The time to embrace Blind Confidence is NOW. Your life is a precious gift, and you have the power to shape it with courage and determination. You have the responsibility to help others you know and love to shape their lives, too.

Do not let uncertainty hold you back any longer. As I share with all of my clients and teams I train, it is time to shift your perspective, elevate your thinking, and activate more options in your life.

Blind Confidence will shift your perspective, elevate your thinking and activate more options in your life. ~Mindy Nelson

---

I invite you to join a growing movement of individuals transforming their lives through Blind Confidence. Whether you seek to improve your relationships, advance your career, or find the courage to pursue your dreams, Blind Confidence can be your guiding light.

To learn more about allowing Blind Confidence™, stay in touch with Mindy by email: mindy.nelson@vitalrevelations.com; visit www.VitalRevelations.com or on LinkedIn at www.LinkedIn.com/in/MindyNelson.

Do not wait for the perfect moment to start your journey. The path to a more confident, fulfilling life begins with a single step. Trust yourself. You got this. Blind Confidence empowers you to achieve your dreams and make a lasting impact. Remember, your unique contribution to the world is waiting to be discovered.

Embrace Blind Confidence, and let it guide you towards the extraordinary life you deserve.

References

Brach, T. (2003). *Radical Acceptance: Embracing Your Life With the Heart of a Buddha*. Bantam.

Brown, B. (2012). *Daring Greatly: How the Courage to Be Vulnerable Transforms the Way We Live, Love, Parent, and Lead*. Gotham Books.

Clear, J. (2018). *Atomic Habits: An Easy & Proven Way to Build Good Habits & Break Bad Ones*. Avery.

Ferriss, T. (2016). *Tools of Titans: The Tactics, Routines, and Habits of Billionaires, Icons, and World-Class Performers*. Houghton Mifflin Harcourt.

Gilbert, E. (2015). *Big Magic: Creative Living Beyond Fear*. Riverhead Books.

Neck, C. P., Houghton, J. D., & Murray, E. L. (2023). *Organizational Behavior* (3rd ed.). SAGE Publications, Inc. (US). https://bookshelf.vitalsource.com/books/9781071854457.

Neff, K. (2011). *Self-Compassion: The Proven Power of Being Kind to Yourself*. William Morrow.

Robbins, M. (2017). *The 5 Second Rule: Transform Your Life, Work, and Confidence with Everyday Courage*. Savio Republic.

Tolle, E. (2004). *The Power of Now: A Guide to Spiritual Enlightenment*. New World Library.

Smith, J. (2022). *Why Has Nobody Told Me This Before?* Harper.

Mindy Nelson

Mindy Nelson, MBA, FACHE, is an accomplished healthcare executive with over two decades of experience in operations, sales, and marketing. Her career includes working with prestigious global brands such as Accenture, Dell, IBM, Johnson & Johnson, and PwC, and she is currently at Guidehouse. Mindy has built over $480 million in partnerships, solutions, and products as an international speaker, trusted advisor, and trainer.

Mindy's expertise extends to serving hospitals, healthcare systems, and health/wellness practices. She has worked with numerous renowned health systems, including Advocate, Emory, Hospital Corporation of America, Johns Hopkins Health System, Piedmont, and Stanford Health Systems. Her experience spans from launching individual health businesses to collaborating with large, nationally recognized health systems and their boards and executives.

Mindy's educational background includes an MBA and BS from Arizona State University, a Certification in Digital Marketing from Cornell, and a Communication Certification from Harvard. She is currently pursuing a doctorate in Industrial Organizational Psychology at Walden University. Her professional involvement includes the Georgia HIMSS Board and College of Healthcare Executives, Georgia

Chapter. In addition to her professional achievements, Mindy serves as Vice President of the Atlanta Chi Omega Alumnae Board.

Mindy is passionate about empowering women to achieve financial independence, advance their education, boost their confidence, and elevate their career opportunities. She resides with her family in Milton, Georgia.

Connect with Mindy at mindy.nelson@vitalrevelations.com; visit www.VitalRevelations.com or www.linkedin.com/in/mindynelson.

CHAPTER 12

The Daily Decision to Shine

Molly Mahoney

This chapter is dedicated to my kiddos Frank and Charleston. Their courage, creativity, and commitment blows my mind every day.

Why Choose Confidence?

Confidence is the cornerstone of personal growth and success. It's the key that unlocks your potential and allows you to pursue your dreams with determination and resilience.

Confidence empowers you to face challenges head-on, make bold decisions, and stand up for your beliefs.

Without confidence, even the most talented individuals can falter, held back by self-doubt and fear.

Confidence is not just about believing in yourself; it's about taking action, pushing through barriers, and inspiring others to do the same.

It's about creating a ripple effect of positivity and strength that can transform lives and communities.

As you read this chapter, I'll take you through the 3 Keys to Unlocking Your Confidence: Courage, Creativity, and Commitment.

And, since ACTION leads to confidence, at the end of each section you'll find an action step that you can put into practice right away!

Hold onto your hats and glasses! We're about to unlock your inner awesome and elevate it so you can change the world!

Step #1: COURAGE: The Foundation for a Confident Life

"Be who you are and say what you feel, because those who mind don't matter, and those who matter don't mind." ~Bernard M. Baruch

---

Courage is the bedrock of confidence. It takes courage to face fears, step out of your comfort zone, and stand up for yourself.

As we embark on this journey of **choosing confidence**, it's important to recognize that courage doesn't mean the absence of fear.

It also doesn't mean taking action despite the fear.

It means taking action BECAUSE of the fear.

What if you could use your fear as a springboard?

Start to recognize fear as an indicator that it's time to MOVE!

Something that reminds you... oh - this means I'm onto something big!

What if you got to think...

"Hmmmm, when I feel fear - I get to use it as a slingshot that will catapult me even further into the future!"

142

One of the greatest barriers to confidence is the fear of being judged.

When I was first building my career, I couldn't get the fear of being seen as "too fancy" or "stuck up" out of my head.

This worry that others will think less of us if we shine too brightly is a common struggle many face.

But remember, those who matter won't mind, and those who mind don't matter!

Choosing confidence means acknowledging these fears and moving forward anyway.

There have been times over the years when I felt the need to dim my light because others thought I was "silly" or "too much."

Ever felt that way?

Leading a large public facing social media based community, I get the gift of facing this fear often.

And let me tell you - imposter syndrome creeps up!

Some people don't like this term... but it makes it easier for us to talk about when we give it a name.

And, it is a huge part of pursuing a creative career or building a business.

Imposter syndrome is often triggered by real-life incidents. It's based on something that we see as "proof" that we are "less than."

When I first started helping others use video in their business, I had a few not-so-nice people make some not-so-nice comments on my videos. Now I know that was a sign that I had made it, but it was a little hard to process back then.

I was reminded of just how tricky it can be when someone turns down an offer or flat-out criticizes what you felt was some of your best work. It was a perfect example of one of those moments that can cause your imposter syndrome gremlins to creep up.

So, in an effort to help you know you aren't alone, I posted a video about the three most embarrassing moments on Facebook™ Live. It was a funny video where I shared real live video fails, warning others so they could avoid these mishaps. I also mentioned a Facebook™ Live Masterclass in the video.

The video had a great response with loads of views, comments, and likes, until the haters showed up.

Comments like "YOU HAVE A LISP AND YOU NEED TO SEE ME!!!" or "YOU ARE SPEAKING WAY TOO FAST TO TEACH A MASTERCLASS!!" and even "FIX YOUR LIPSTICK???" flooded in.

AND... when you haven't decided to make Confidence a Choice, comments like this can cause your imposter syndrome to flare up big time.

I came up with a way for you to love the ickiness that comes up with trolls or imposter syndrome in four easy steps.

It's called the FFTT method. Here is how to overcome imposter syndrome in four easy steps:

1. **Face It**: Recognize that something happened that makes you feel small, or icky, or bummed, or even angry.

2. **Feel It**: Allow yourself to go into the negative feelings, even comparisonitis.

3. **Twist It**: Ask yourself, "How can I turn this into a positive?" How can I use this as a teaching moment to help others?

4. **Thank It**: Once you twist it, thank it! Be grateful for the opportunity to grow!

Honestly... I LOVE comments like this now. We even turned one of my biggest hater comments into a meme making fun of me and it is the BEST.

You can see it at www.molly.live/trolls. It's so funny!!

Once I realized the importance of standing up for my joy and shining my light regardless of others' opinions... everything changed.

I now know... when I stand up to these negative comments in a way that is lighthearted and playful, confidently owning my authenticity... it empowers others to gain the confidence to shine their own light!

ACTION STEPS:

1. **Face Your Fears**: Identify specific fears that hold you back and take small steps to confront them. Start with low-risk situations and gradually move to more challenging ones.

2. **Positive Affirmations**: Use affirmations to build your courage. Remind yourself daily that you are capable, worthy, and strong.

3. **Celebrate Small Wins DAILY**: Recognize and celebrate your achievements, no matter how small. Each victory builds your courage and confidence. In our coaching programs, we always start with wins... it unlocks your ability to see the wins that are on the way!

STEP #2: CREATIVITY: Your Weird is Your Superpower

"You are your best thing." ~Toni Morrison

Creativity is not just for artists; it's for everyone.

It involves thinking outside the box, finding unique solutions, and expressing oneself authentically.

Authenticity Over Gimmicks

I once saw an ad with a woman comparing making offers to streaking.

It made me laugh and also made me wonder if we really need to resort to such extremes to stand out.

The key to unlocking creativity is actually authenticity.

When you allow yourself to really tap into who YOU are... creativity flows.

Confidence in being authentic and connected to your truth Is far more effective than gimmicks.

Your business doesn't need to be the "naked cowboy." Stand out by telling the truth and your community will thank you for it!

Owning Your "Weird"

Really - Your Weird is your Superpower.

It's the one thing others can't copy. Confidence comes from embracing your uniqueness and understanding that what makes you different is your strength.

Whether it's a love for vintage fashion, a quirky hobby, or an unconventional approach to business, these unique traits are your superpowers.

This is so random - but I made brussels sprouts a key part of our brand, proving that anything is possible!

Four people have sent me the same dishtowel that says, "Every Day I'm Brusslin."

When people go to restaurants, they send me photos of their sprouts. When they find a good recipe - I'm the one they DM.

This unconventional idea underscores the limitless possibilities when you believe in yourself and your vision.

How did I end up weaving in brussels sprouts as a part of my full brand - it all started with a quesadilla.

The Quesadilla of Awesome

Imagine a quesadilla... Everyone loves them, right?

A soft, warm tortilla that can be filled with any and every ingredient you can think of.

And that's the beauty of them - you ask five people to make a quesadilla and each person will give you their own version!

YOU are the quesadilla and all your quirks and perks are the ingredients that make up YOU.

And so you are going to make a list of the 20 things that make YOU amazing.

Here's how you can create your own Quesadilla of Awesome:

- **Skills**: What are you really good at? These can be professional skills or personal talents.
- **Appearance**: What are the unique aspects of how you present yourself to the world?
- **Activities**: What do you love to do? Think about your hobbies and interests.
- **Values**: What do you stand for? What are the core beliefs that drive your actions?
- **Eat**: What are your favorite foods? This might seem silly, but it's a great conversation starter and makes you more relatable.

These ingredients make up your unique Quesadilla of Awesome. When you embrace and celebrate these traits, you'll find that people are drawn to your authenticity and the real you.

Play the "What If" Game?

What if you fully embraced your weird?

What if you allowed your creativity to flourish without fear of judgment?

What if you showed up as your true self, unapologetically?

The possibilities are endless when you decide to own your uniqueness.

The world needs your unique voice, your perspective, and your creative solutions.

Practical Tips:

- **Identify Your Unique Traits**: Make a list of what makes you unique. Follow the framework from above. Celebrate these qualities and think about how you can incorporate them into your daily life and business.

- **Be Authentic in Your Branding**: Ensure that your personal and business branding reflects your true self. Authenticity resonates more deeply with others and builds lasting connections.

- **Practice PLAY**: Look for creative solutions to problems. Approach challenges with an open mind and a willingness to experiment with new ideas.

Step #3: COMMITMENT: The Glue That Holds It All Together

"The willingness to show up changes us; it makes us a little braver each time." ~Brene Brown

---

Commitment is the glue that holds courage and creativity together.

It's about making a consistent, daily choice to pursue your goals with determination and resilience.

Daily Practices for Joy

To maintain commitment, recognize the joy that exists every day and keep a record of it. Years ago my grandma Bobbie and I used to send each other our Daily Joys via email. It was such an amazing practice. Once she passed, I started keeping a "Joy Journal" by my bed and recorded the "joys" of my day every night before heading to sleep.

Even in times that seem dire, finding one small moment of good keeps you on track.

Sometimes we run these little joy challenges in my free community on social media. Keep an eye out if you want to join us! Or, should I say... joy'n us. LOL

Accountability Partners

Find someone who will hold you accountable. It's easy to get sucked into the drama of moments that pull us away from the good.

Having a trusted friend or coach who keeps you on track is essential. My grandma and I sent those emails to each other every day sharing one joy, no matter what. Even if it was just a great cup of coffee, we were forced to share that joy because we didn't want to let each other down.

Filling Up Your Cup

Years ago I had the chance to interview Daniel Day-Lewis. It was an amazing experience. I asked him how he managed to balance his career with his personal life.

His answer shook me to my core.

First of all - he looked into my SOUL and then in his very Daniel Day-Lewisy voice he said...

"This career will scoop the life out of you! If you don't set aside time to fill up, you will not survive."

Whoa.

This is true for any commitment. If you're making a full-force commitment to giving good and spreading joy, you must make time to fill up so you have enough to give.

Commit to yourself and your own joy before giving goodness to the world.

One way I do this is by ending my day early on Wednesdays. The afternoon is set aside for two things. Learning and Creating Magic. It's an amazing way to make sure I've filled my cup so I have the energy to make confidence a choice.

Embracing Resilience

Resilience is a key component of confidence. It's about bouncing back from setbacks and using those experiences to grow stronger.

Now that I've become an expert at turning messes into magic, I've started calling these opportunities Big Sparkly Boulders.

One of my most vivid examples involves a rather embarrassing audition. Picture this: you're at an audition for a huge Broadway show. The room is filled with 36 triple-threat dancers—stellar singers, astounding actors, and fierce dancers. And, there's you!

The choreography is perfect for you stylistically. You have this callback in the bag. The choreographer explains that there is an 8-count of improvisation in the middle of this dance combo.

He wants you to pretend you're a USO dancer in the 1940s...

DRESSED LIKE A TURKEY!

After you get over the initial shock, you feel that bubbly excitement in your chest—you know you got this!

When it comes to your turn, you kick your face and exclaim, "Bkak! Bkak!," thrusting your chest like a turkey. As you do, you slowly realize that your 1940's vintage top feels a little looser than it did when the audition started. You look down and, to your horror, your shirt has completely ripped open, leaving you exposed not only to the 36 triple threats but also to the full creative team (director, casting director, choreographer)!

In that split second, you have a choice to make.

You can:

A. Scream and run out of the room never to be seen again.

B. Laugh uncontrollably, mortified, and unable to finish the dance combination.

C. Cover your chest and give that number the best energy you've got, standing with confidence, accepting the fact that everyone in that room is mortified for you, so you don't need to be mortified yourself!

What would you do?

When this happened to me at an audition for South Pacific on Broadway, I took a split-second pause and decided to keep going. I finished the combination with more pizzazz than ever.

When we ended in our own pose, I went straight to the splits and gave it a big TADA!!

I thought, if there's ever a time I'll get a callback, this is it!

Sadly, it was a required call, so NO ONE got a callback.

However, at an audition for the same casting director a few months later, I reminded her of the story. I walked in and said, "Hi, I am Molly Mahoney, the girl whose top ripped at the South Pacific audition!"

She instantly threw her hands in the air, screamed for joy, and told me it was one of her favorite audition moments to date.

That was the perfect proof in my positivity pudding!

ACTION STEPS:

1. **Keep a Joy Journal**: Record daily moments of joy and review them regularly to maintain a positive mindset.

2. **Get a Resilience Buddy**: Find someone who will challenge you to step out of your comfort zone and support you when you fall.

3. **Schedule Self-Care**: Make self-care a non-negotiable part of your routine. Whether it's a hobby, exercise, or simply relaxing, prioritize activities that recharge you.

Conclusion: Choose Confidence

Choosing confidence is an ongoing journey that requires courage, creativity, and commitment. By facing your fears, embracing your uniqueness, and committing to daily practices that bring joy, you can cultivate confidence in every aspect of your life.

Remember, confidence is a choice you make every day. It's about showing up, standing out, and shining brightly, no matter what challenges or Big Sparkly Boulders come your way.

As we continue this journey together, know that confidence is not just about personal growth; it's about creating a ripple effect that empowers others. Together, we can build a world where everyone has the confidence to shine their light and pursue their dreams.

And, at times, you may not feel that you have the courage to muster the confidence, or you may get stuck in finding ways to put your confidence-building muscles into practice mode.

So, I've created a guide that makes it super easy to communicate with confidence even if you aren't quite there yet.

"Confident Conversations: 17 Secrets to Command Any Room" is designed to give you practical tools and insights that you can apply immediately. Whether you're preparing for a big presentation, networking at an event, or simply wanting to express yourself more effectively, this guide will help you take those crucial steps towards becoming the confident, empowered individual you are meant to be.

Connect with Molly at www.mollymahoney.com.

The world is waiting for your light to shine!

Molly Mahoney

Molly Mahoney (known as The Prepared Performer) is a Business Growth Strategist who specializes in creating authentic content and leveraging organic social media, AI, and automation marketing to sky-rocket client sales.

After creating a video that reached one million people organically, she developed her signature "Go Live And Monetize" method. It combines her social media expertise, talent for scaling one-on-one relationships, and 20 years of performance experience on stages from New York to Las Vegas. Her most recent viral video hit a reach of 39 million! Molly has been featured by Be.live, ManyChat, Social Media Marketing World, Traffic & Conversion Summit, Perry Belcher, Rich Schefren's Steal our Winners, Inc magazine, Forbes, Entrepreneur and more.

Her children's book Finding My Awesome allows kiddos of all ages to celebrate their unique sense of awesome and live a life of confidence and joy.

When she's not helping her clients attract a flood of leads, you can find her singing jazz with her bass-playing husband or teaching her kids to #stand4joy from their home in California.

Grab your free copy of Molly's **"Confident Conversations: 17 Secrets to Command Any Room"** and start your journey today at www.chooseconfidence.com/mollygift.

CHAPTER 13

Throwing Self-Doubt to the Dogs

Nancy Quintana-Reyes

This chapter is dedicated to the countless individuals who have entrusted me as a part of their journey with their dogs. Your trust has been both an honor and a privilege. Thank you for allowing me to be a part of your lives.

The Beginning

Failure is a powerful teacher, and boy, nothing has been truer in my life. It was a hot day in Austin, Texas, in 1985, and there he was, a 12-pound ball of black fluff hiding under the table. The last pup left. I wondered why he was the last one, but it didn't matter—I was already smitten. Off we went, embarking on our new relationship. What a journey it was. Winston, my Black Chow, became my teacher in love, patience, tolerance, happiness, and sadness.

Almost immediately, Winston revealed his distress about people and dogs. He was anxious and fearful, using biting to navigate his world. Our journey was filled with challenges—he bit almost everyone in my family, and I felt overwhelmed by his aggressive behavior.

Winston ignited my journey into understanding dog behavior. I always loved dogs, but I didn't truly understand them. Back then, dog training was different, and discussions about dog behavior were rare.

Winston was afraid of people, and I couldn't comprehend why. His fear seemed like an insurmountable barrier. At the time, training methods were heavily compulsion-based, which only exacerbated Winston's fear. I realized that using force to address fear was not going to work. I had to muster the confidence to tell the trainers I was working with that their methods weren't helping and, in fact, were making things worse.

Dog trainers are often seen as authoritative experts, but the unregulated nature of the industry means many lack proper knowledge. Despite this, I was determined to find a better way to help Winston.

Years of breaking up dog fights and protecting him from biting others became my reality. My quest to improve Winston's life was relentless. Each failure felt like a personal defeat because I couldn't make things better for us.

Through the trials with Winston, I learned that understanding and compassion, not force, are the keys to helping our dogs. With every failure trying to help this dog that I adored, he put me on the path of learning and adapting to this ever-changing situation.

Passion Ignited

Winston and I had a good life together, challenging but good. I kept him and everyone else safe by giving him skills to deal with his world and not putting him in situations that made him anxious. After Winston's passing, I jumped in with both feet to help other dogs avoid the struggles Winston and I faced. I began working with different rescues, conducting evaluations, home visits, and fostering. Through fostering, I truly learned about dog behavior and how to help.

My first rescue was Molly, an 8-pound Miniature Pinscher who was eight years old. Her owners had to rehome her because they had a baby. Every day, Molly would wait by the front door for her family to return. It was so sad to watch her tiny body standing there, eyes filled with hope that today would be the day they came back for her. She did this for two weeks; it was heart-wrenching. She couldn't understand why the only home she knew was gone, and now she was with a stranger, facing a disrupted life.

There were days when it made me so angry—how could someone just dispose of an animal because it wasn't convenient? The depth of Molly's heartbreak was palpable. Watching her mourn the loss of her family, feeling her confusion and sadness, tore at my soul. Her story is not unique; it's a devastating reality for many pets.

It was then that I decided to dedicate my life to helping people better understand dogs. I wanted to prevent arbitrary decisions that could drastically impact a dog's life. People move, have babies, and undergo life changes, often not realizing the emotional turmoil these decisions can cause their pets. They don't see the broken hearts they leave behind or the confusion and fear that consume these loyal companions.

The emotional toll of such disruptions is immense. For Molly, every day was a battle to understand her new reality. The sense of abandonment she felt was something no animal should ever have to endure. This experience with Molly fueled my passion for helping dogs. I realized that education and compassion were key to preventing such heartbreak.

I wanted to be the voice for those like Molly who couldn't speak for themselves, to ensure that their lives weren't tossed aside when circumstances changed.

Molly's story is a testament to the importance of resilience and passion. Despite the pain, she gradually adapted to her new life, and her spirit began to heal. Her journey inspired me to pursue learning more about dog training and behavior. My passion for helping those animals who could not help themselves became the powerful force that drove me to want to make a difference.

Through my work, I strive to show others the profound impact of their decisions on their pets' lives. I advocate for patience, understanding, and finding ways to integrate pets into new life circumstances. Molly's heartbreak ignited a fire in me—a commitment to help dogs and their owners navigate challenges together. This passion, combined with resilience, can transform lives, ensuring that no dog has to endure the pain of feeling unwanted or abandoned.

During this time, I was a successful mortgage banker, thriving in my career. However, my true passion lay elsewhere. I dedicated my spare time to fostering dogs and delving deeper into the world of dog training. I conducted temperament testing and evaluations for various rescues in our area, fostering many dogs over the years. Balancing my demanding job with my commitment to helping dogs meant working almost day and night. Yet, with each passing day, my desire to work with and help dogs grew stronger. The fulfillment I found in making a difference in their lives was unparalleled, further fueling a passion that only intensified as time went on.

Dog Training: My Calling

As I did more fostering, I also started doing more training and found that I really loved and had a natural talent for it. I got a part-time job as a dog trainer and thoroughly enjoyed what I was doing. It was at that moment I found my calling—helping people with their dogs and improving dogs' lives. It was very clear and very quick. I started training part-time for many years and loved every minute of it. I enjoy people and love dogs, making it the perfect combination.

However, dog training is far from perfect. Our society has many old myths and misconceptions about dogs, how to train them, and what to train them. Helping people unlearn these outdated notions and open their minds to new methodologies is a significant challenge. The study of animal behavior is still relatively new, and while more studies are being done on dogs, their behavior, health, and overall well-being, the basic premises are still evolving.

As I approached my 40th birthday, I wondered if there was more to life than just working in corporate America and making money. I always knew I wanted to start a business but didn't know what it would be. I found immense joy in dog training, being present with the dogs, and making a positive impact. So, I decided to start a dog training business. I put the idea out into the universe, believing that if it was meant to be, everything would fall into place effortlessly.

I was at a crossroads between my full-time bill-paying job and going into the unknown world of dog training, knowing that financially it would never be the same. My husband knew it, too. While he supported me completely, he was sad about the enormous change in our financial situation. But he encouraged me to go for it. It was the most difficult decision of my life, leaving a secure situation and moving into the vast unknown.

In October 2004, For Your K9 was founded in a facility in Schiller Park, Illinois. With a wealth of marketing knowledge and a passion for dogs, I was ready to make a difference, relying on faith, passion, and persistence.

I had a plan and learned that plans need to be flexible. I needed to develop the skills and adjust as things moved along. I HAD to be confident in my decisions and be okay with the outcomes. Many outcomes were great while others not so much. Early on, I fretted about my bad decisions. One of those such decisions was the expansion of my business too soon. I added another building we called the Annex, which put the business on the brink of bankruptcy—spending too much money in setting things up and not being able to generate enough income from classes to sustain it. After a while, I was able to reflect and learn from the poor decisions and not repeat them. Reflecting, I also wanted to learn from what I did right.

There is always a way to make things work; you just have to look and ask for help. Help is always there! I promise. And sometimes, in the most unexpected places. Being upfront and honest pays off big. Who would ask the landlord for help when they owed so much money? Me! After the Annex fiasco, I had to pivot quickly if I wanted For Your K9 to survive. The landlord and I worked out a deal we could both live with and on we went. Believing there is always a way to work things out became my driving force.

Getting Better: The Learning

Since dog training is not regulated, I had to figure out how to get even better at understanding dogs. At this point, I had several years of rescue experience, but I still felt I needed to know more. I was fortunate to find great, super-intelligent mentors along the way. I spent many weekends driving to seminars and workshops, learning as much as possible, investing money and time in getting better at my job, my passion.

I knew that the key to all the homeless dogs, dog abuse, and bad relationships with dogs was understanding and education. Understanding dog behavior is crucial for a harmonious relationship between dogs and their owners. Many behavioral issues stem from misunderstandings or miscommunications between dogs and their humans. Dogs, like humans, have complex emotions and needs that must be met for them to thrive. Recognizing the signs of anxiety, fear, and stress in dogs can significantly improve their quality of life. Living a more harmonious life together includes providing dogs with skills in dealing with their owner's lifestyle and giving owners the skills to understand why dogs behave the way they do.

Staying True

Can your passion coexist with your profession?

How do you stay confident when there are mistakes and roadblocks everywhere you turn?

Knowing that there's an answer out there somewhere that needs to be found in another approach or another way to look at it is the answer. For example, when Winston was going through all of that aggression, dog medication was not as common as it is now. I had a wonderful veterinarian who suggested using estrogen to help deal with Winston's issues. We had mild success with that approach, but it was better than nothing.

There have been more challenges with the different facilities over the years. We have survived several flooding episodes, fires, cats peeing on the ceiling (seriously, that happened), and terrible neighbors.

These challenges involved me moving the business three times, each with its own set of hurdles, testing my resilience and adaptability at every turn.

One of my biggest challenges was a beloved friend and trainer leaving the business. We worked closely together for six years, THE most difficult years. We worked so hard almost nonstop for all six years. I was so focused on getting and keeping the business up and running that I ignored the mental and physical toll it took on both of us, and one day she was gone. I felt as if the world was coming to an end, betrayed, and just plain sad. I wasn't sure I could keep going. I figured it out, and I had to pivot AGAIN during a very difficult time.

One way I reflect is by journaling the pros and cons of the situation. It helps clarify things, and I always make decisions after I sleep on them. I learned the hard way to not make decisions when your feelings are running high.

I've always had a knack for persistence, constantly seeking solutions and finding unique ways to resolve problems. If one approach doesn't work, I look for another, and that's where my confidence comes from.

If we can't solve something one way, there's always another perspective to consider. This mindset translates directly to my approach in dog training and business. If one methodology doesn't work, we try another. It's about understanding the root cause of the issue and then figuring out the best way to address it. Through this persistent and flexible approach, we can overcome challenges and help dogs and their owners achieve harmony.

Twenty years have flown by, a whirlwind of challenges and triumphs. Reflecting on this journey, I realize how much I've grown, both as a business owner and as an individual. I believe that everything happens for a reason. People may leave, but often when they return, the bonds are stronger than ever. The trainer leaving the business needed to happen in order for me to step into my confidence so my business could run better than before.

When I first started, I yearned for guidance and mentorship, a beacon of support to help navigate the complexities of running and developing a business. However, I soon discovered there was no blueprint for what I was building—no existing business like mine from which to seek advice, no mentor to answer my questions or offer feedback. I had to carve out my own path, relying on sheer determination and perseverance to figure things out.

Every obstacle became a lesson, every setback a steppingstone. The absence of a clear roadmap forced me to innovate and adapt, honing my skills and deepening my understanding of both business and canine behavior. Looking back, the lack of a predefined path was a blessing in disguise, pushing me to become resilient, resourceful, and confident in my vision. Through ALL of it, my vision of helping people better understand dogs NEVER changed. Why did I keep going, one may ask? It's hard to explain, but I just knew I could help. If I could change the relationship between one dog and one human, then that human would have a different relationship with subsequent dogs, AND other people could see how great it can be, and lives of more dogs would be better.

Embracing the Journey

Sometimes I look back at where I came from—the daughter of im-mlgrant parents to a successful business owner—and I still can't believe it. One dog started this amazing journey. Entrepreneurship can be a lonely journey, one that few truly understand. The drive, the late nights, the constant balancing act—it often feels isolating. Amidst this solitude, you can find strength. One of the key secrets to my success has been the confidence to embrace change, make bold decisions, venture down uncharted paths, and try new things in my business, even if it meant facing failure.

Dog training, entrepreneurship, and much of life is an evolving process. Flexibility, adaptability, and passion are critical to any success. Each setback has brought invaluable lessons, helping us make better, more informed decisions as we move forward. This journey, with all its ups and downs, has not only shaped my business but also sculpted my character, teaching me resilience, innovation, and the true meaning of perseverance.

Looking back over the past two decades, I am filled with a profound sense of accomplishment. The challenges, the lonely moments, the victories—all have contributed to the tapestry of my entrepreneurial journey. Here's to the next 20 years, embracing the unknown with the same courage and confidence that has brought me this far.

What I Have Learned

- Your failures do not define you; they shape your path to success.

- Equip yourself with knowledge and empathy to tackle challenges effectively.
- Sometimes you just need to put your intentions out there and trust the process.
- Confidence comes from knowing that there are multiple solutions to any problem. Stay flexible and open-minded.
- Your journey is a testament to your strength and determination.

This is the one thing I did that helped immensely.

Dedicate a notebook or digital document as your Learning Confidence Journal. Each day, spend 10-15 minutes reflecting on your learning progress.

- Write down at least one new thing you learned that day. This reinforces your learning and acknowledges your progress.
- Note any difficulties you encountered and how you addressed them. Reflect on what you can do differently next time.
- List any positive experiences or successes related to your learning. This could be mastering a new concept or successfully applying what you learned.

As you go through difficult times or meet milestones, pull out that notebook and see where you have been and where you are headed.

This journey laid the foundation of For Your K9 and the many programs past, present, and future. We empower dog owners to build stronger, healthier relationships with their pets. Together we can turn challenges into triumphs, ensuring a better life for our dogs and ourselves.

Nancy Reyes

With three decades of professional experience, Nancy Reyes, CNWI is a dedicated dog trainer whose journey began with a childhood fascination for animals. Her fascination turned into her now working with animals that have a variety of behavior issues, giving them the ability to live a happy life.

In 2004, Nancy took the leap and established For Your K9 Inc., a thriving hub offering a diverse range of classes including Puppy, Basic Obedience, Agility, Barn Hunt, Rally, and Nose Work in Elmhurst, Illinois. She has worked extensively with a wide range of behavior issues from aggression to separation anxiety. At the heart of Nancy's training philosophy lies the belief in nurturing the bond between people and their dogs through effective communication and mutual respect.

Nancy holds multiple roles within the canine nose work community, serving as a Certifying Official and Certified Instructor (CNWI) for NACSW (National Association of Canine Scent Work), a CPE (Canine Performance Events) Scent Work judge, and a CWAGS (Canine Work and Games) judge. She has mentored many scent work instructors locally and internationally in person and virtually.

Nancy is an international speaker and presenter on dog behavior and nose work. She has written articles for various breed magazines and conducts webinars for various groups. She is a certified Mental Management Instructor, coaching dog-handler teams to achieve their performance goals across different dog sports.

Connect with Nancy at www.foryourk9.com and nancy@foryourk9.com.

CHAPTER 14

From Fear to Freedom: Redefining Confidence and Taking Action

Shana Brownell

To my husband, whose humor, mischief, and relentless prodding pushed me to face my fears and eventually find true confidence. Thanks for reminding me as often as needed that "No" is a complete sentence and for flagging my ADHD, without which I might never have made it this far.

It has been estimated that 70% of people experience imposter syndrome at some point in their career. For high achievers, it's even more common.

Unfortunately, the personal growth, self-help, and coaching industries often promote quick-fixes and surface-level solutions that don't create lasting change. These methods may create fleeting moments of confidence or inspiration, but ignore the deep-seated impact of past trauma and the vital role of the nervous system, leaving many people feeling stuck and hopeless despite their best efforts. Or worse, when they don't work at all, or only work temporarily, they foster a downward spiral of shame and self-doubt that further erodes their confidence, something I have experienced firsthand.

For years, I knew I was here to make a difference and dreamed of building my own business. While working full time, I studied business and created side hustles as a photographer, copywriter, and web designer. However, I struggled to spend much time on any of these while working and none were even close to replacing the income from my job or felt like my true calling.

In 2018, when I suddenly lost my job, it felt like the perfect time to finally get focused and become the successful entrepreneur I had always talked about being. A year later, I hadn't created anything.

Sound familiar?

In fact, despite spending thousands of dollars on a private business coach, I still didn't even know WHAT I wanted to create. I worried about starting and trapping myself in the "wrong" business and was too afraid of failing or being judged or ridiculed to even begin to show up visibly online. I kept telling myself that once I had more confidence and clarity I would be ready. Meanwhile, we were in debt, out of savings, and I had to go back to work having failed to create anything of significance.

This was one of my lowest moments, and one of the most important. I KNEW I was here for something more and wasn't ready to give up on my dreams but, for the first time in my life, I saw that the things I pointed to for years as the reason I didn't have a wildly successful business were NOT the problem. Being busy and having a full-time job were never what was keeping me from working for myself. Despite years of therapy, self-help books, courses, and even paying an expensive private business coach, I still was not YET the person that could make those dreams a reality.

I knew there MUST be a missing piece and I went back to work determined to find it.

Fast-forward a few years, and not only did I find the missing pieces to untangle my own painful patterns of self-doubt, overwhelm, procrastination, and more--by combining more than 10 years of study and experience in personal development with in-depth training and mentorship from The Institute for Trauma and Psychological Safety and the Institute for Woman-Centered Coaching, Development, and Leadership, I learned how to fast-track that journey for others.

After working with those organizations, I launched ROARify, a successful coaching business I previously couldn't even see as a possibility. I now get to support others to become their most brilliant, badass selves and create a life that truly lights them up. I co-authored a bestselling book, The Habits Code. And I have spoken online to groups with thousands of people about topics like stepping into confidence and visibility. Today, I not only have a clear vision for the life I'm creating, I have the confidence and support to take powerful, exciting, and sometimes scary action to create it.

And the best part is, I'm living the purpose I had sensed for so long - helping others to quickly and permanently break free from shame, self-doubt, and patterns that have held them back for years or decades so they can own their power and become unstoppable in creating a life they love.

I know how painful it can be to feel stuck in fear, overwhelm, anxiety, and self-doubt. To try... and try.... but feel like you're never getting any traction.

And I know what it's like to be on the other side, to be your own best friend and cheerleader, to have a clear vision and the courage and confidence to pursue it.

I want this for everyone and am honored and excited to share with you some key shifts that can finally take you from feeling stuck and stagnant to being in action to create the life you really want.

If you know you're meant for more but feel stuck at the starting line, spinning your wheels, getting nowhere, and wishing for someone... ANYONE... to give you the clarity you've been looking for and the confidence you need, or you're tired of searching for answers and wishing you just had the confidence to go all in on your dreams, this chapter is for you.

Let's dive in.

What is Confidence, Really?

Do you find yourself waiting to feel confident and ready before taking action on your goals? Watching opportunities pass by because you don't feel ready? Seeing others around you that seem to have it all together while you feel paralyzed by overwhelm, fear, and self-doubt, searching for the confidence you need?

We often think that confidence means not having fear of whatever it is we're doing, that when we're confident, we can go all in knowing we've got this, that we will feel confident when we know we can be successful or sure that people will like us.

That is not confidence.

And worse, approaching your dreams and goals from that perspective can actually keep you stuck and erode your confidence rather than building it. I know, because that's what happened to me.

There was a time when I failed (or failed to get started) so many times that the only thing I had confidence in was my ability to fail. I saw others around me thriving in their relationships and showing up powerfully in their businesses, but I felt stuck and powerless to create that in my own life.

I was stuck in shame and eventually my confidence had eroded so much that I mostly stopped setting goals at all. If I did have goals, I damn sure didn't tell anyone about them because part of me didn't trust that I could achieve them (especially if they required me to be visible). I just knew that I would fail (yet again) to take the actions I needed to, or that even if I did take them, they probably wouldn't work. And when that happened, I didn't want anyone but me to know that I had failed... again.

I felt broken and alone.

Eventually, though, I found a community of growth-oriented women where I could connect deeply and share my struggles. When I did, I discovered that all the things I was feeling and experiencing, all the things I thought were wrong with me, were NOT unique to me. They were not proof that something was wrong with me or that I had to "fix" myself. They were just part of being human.

This realization finally freed me from the isolation and downward shame spiral I'd been in for years and I was finally able to start healing and growing. And in the process, I learned what confidence really is.

The truth is that things are always going to be uncomfortable, maybe even scary, the first time you do them. Some things may still feel that way the 100th time you do them. Public speaking anyone?

Getting rid of the fear is not, and can never be, the path to confidence. It's time to let go of the myth that having confidence and moving forward means getting rid of fear or discomfort about the thing, feeling ready, or knowing the outcome in advance.

It's time to stop chasing certainty, clarity, or perfection believing that once we have those, then we will be confident.

It is time to redefine confidence and our relationship to it.

So, what is confidence, really?

Authentic confidence comes from self-trust, resilience, and adaptability, from knowing you have the ability to navigate any potential outcome—positive or negative. It's the ability to trust in and create safety for yourself, so you can take steps forward in spite of fear and discomfort. When you have that, and you start to take imperfect action, not only do you have the confidence to take on scary, new things, but a lot of things start to feel less scary. You create momentum and your confidence grows and builds on itself almost magically.

How do you create that knowing? How do you cultivate self-trust and resilience and start building REAL confidence? Not the fake it 'til you make it kind, but the deeper kind that unleashes you and makes you unstoppable?

Release Shame

First and foremost, it's time to kick shame to the curb.

If you've struggled with confidence in one or more areas of your life, you might feel like that means something is wrong with you, but the truth is, you're human. Most people struggle with this at some point in at least one area of their life. This is because we all have past painful experiences that, whether we realize it or not, still affect us if we haven't dealt with them.

I mentioned earlier that many self-help programs and techniques fail to create lasting change because they ignore the impact of trauma and past painful experiences and the vital role of the nervous system in shaping our behaviors and confidence.

When I say trauma, you probably think of things like war, natural disasters, abuse, or a sudden loss. While these things certainly are traumatic, the truth is that any experience where you felt unsafe, whether that's physical safety or mental or emotional safety, can be traumatic and get stuck in your body, especially if you felt like you didn't have control. For example, a seemingly small experience like being called on or embarrassed by a teacher when you weren't prepared or

174

being called out at work can lead to feeling unsafe sharing your ideas when you don't know how they'll be received or aren't sure you have the right answer. Perhaps when you were young, your parents fought a lot and you tried to keep the peace and now as an adult, conflict gives you massive anxiety and you often find yourself people-pleasing, denying your needs, and trying to conform.

If you've had any of these experiences—you're human and none of us get through unscathed, so I can say pretty confidently that you have—they may still be affecting you today. Knowing that, I invite you to take another look at any places where you have struggled to feel confident or take action, where you might even know the steps you need to take but haven't been able to get yourself to take them. I invite you to recognize and acknowledge that these areas have been hard because your body and your nervous system are trying to protect you and stop blaming and shaming yourself for the fact that it has felt hard and you haven't been able to feel confident or get traction.

Starting now, you can embrace a new way of being and of relating to your struggles, where you no longer fight against your nervous system and its efforts to keep you safe and instead, learn to partner with it. Old beliefs, patterns, and habits you've labeled as self-sabotage, are really about self-protection, but you can break these habits by gradually expanding what feels safe to your nervous system.

Next, I'll share how to do that, but first, I invite you to pause and reflect on your past struggles.

Action Step: Consider journaling or writing a letter to yourself expressing compassion for your past experiences and expressing understanding and forgiveness for the struggles they've created.

Become BFFs with Your Nervous System

Connecting with and listening to your body and nervous system is crucial for building lasting confidence. Your nervous system is always working to protect you, and it often resists your attempts to reach your goals by shutting you down. To develop real confidence and move towards your goals, you must learn to move forward in ways that get your brain and nervous system on board, instead of trying to overpower or fight against them.

Think of your comfort zone like a rubber band. When you stretch it gradually, it loosens up over time. However, if you stretch it too far, too fast, it snaps. Similarly, stepping too far outside your comfort zone too quickly can lead to overwhelm and retraumatization. Instead, partner with your nervous system by taking small, manageable steps that stretch you just enough to grow but still feel safe. For example, if you want to launch a website but can't seem to get started, give yourself permission to just work on it without launching. If you've built it but don't quite feel ready to launch, share it with one supportive person for feedback.

Your stretch steps don't have to relate directly to your goals. They just have to stretch you a little bit closer to the person you want to become. One way I started to break my own pattern of perfectionism and overanalysis was by taking an online improv class. I chose this because by definition I didn't get to know all the answers before getting started. Nobody did!

That class was an uncomfortable (initially) but safe place to practice showing up even when I didn't feel ready. I was able to embrace imperfection and just do the thing. Through that experience, I learned that things can be messy, uncomfortable, valuable, and even fun all at the same time. And I learned that when my inner critic steps aside, I can be pretty damn creative (and life is a lot more interesting).

Note that you may get stuck in this step by trying to push yourself too far too quickly, leading to overwhelm or retriggering past trauma. To avoid this, stick with steps that push you just beyond your current edge. These small steps may seem tiny and insignificant, but their cumulative impact is HUGE and is key to building your confidence.

Action Step: Consider ways you can create safety for yourself to practice or make progress on something. Identify one or two small steps that can move you towards your goal, or help you practice a skill you want to develop. These steps should stretch you towards your goal but feel safe enough to be doable.

Focus on Action, Prioritize Consistency, and CELEBRATE

Another crucial shift is focusing on what you can control (your actions) rather than on what you can't control (the results those actions may or may not create). There will be times when you get stuck or stopped or feel like you're moving backwards. That is okay, normal, and expected, so give yourself grace when things don't go as planned and challenges arise.

It's tempting to go for big leaps towards your goals, and eventually you can absolutely do that. But first, as you're learning to work with your nervous system and stretch what it can handle, focus on small, doable steps and consistent action, and celebrate each step, even (and especially) when it feels silly to do so.

When I was working to break my own patterns of people-pleasing, overcommitting, and saying yes when I wanted to say no, I celebrated and high-fived with my husband every time I managed to say no or speak up. These were small but critical moments where I chose to show up differently, and celebrating them made them even more significant and memorable to my nervous system, making them easier and more automatic over time.

Stacking up and celebrating small steps and wins builds confidence and, over time, moves you toward the big wins.

Note that you may get stuck here or struggle to stay motivated if you don't see immediate results. One of the best ways to counteract this, set yourself up for long-term success, and make sure that you get back on track when life knocks you off, is to find support.

Action Step: Identify and reach out to a potential support system. This could include a friend, mentor, community group, or coach.

To wrap up, let's review the key shifts discussed in this chapter:

- Redefine confidence (it's about self-trust and resilience, not lack of fear or discomfort).
- Release shame.
- Make friends with your nervous system.
- Take actions that stretch your comfort zone (but don't take you too far outside it too quickly).
- Focus on the actions you can control (not the outcomes you can't).
- Prioritize consistency.
- Celebrate your wins.

To ground this in, I invite you to close your eyes, take a deep breath, and imagine taking one small step towards your goal. As you imagine this, feel the support of your nervous system and feel yourself celebrating this step as a victory. This is how you begin to transform fear and uncertainty into confidence and resilience.

Next Steps

If you feel overwhelmed or doubt that this will work for you, congratulations! That is completely normal. Change can be scary, and old habits can be hard to break. Fortunately, I've got you.

To support you on this journey, I'd like to offer you my Stress Less, Thrive More audio series, available on my website, www.ROARify.com. This series will take you deeper into these steps and help you start building resilience and creating your own personal toolkit for working with your nervous system.

If you're ready for more personalized support, let's connect. Together, we can create a plan that aligns with your unique needs and goals.

As you move forward, remember that you are powerful, resilient, and capable of achieving your dreams. Embrace the journey and keep showing up for yourself. You are worth it!

Shana Brownell

Shana Brownell, founder of ROARify, is a fierce advocate for living authentically and challenging the norm. As a transformational coach, author, and speaker, she's all about genuine conversations, rejecting cliche self-help advice, and addressing real issues with compassion, not sugar coating.

Having deeply applied trauma-informed transformational practices in her own journey, she expertly steers others toward enduring change. With a Masters in Education and over 15 years experience teaching and mentoring others, she targets shame at its roots, fosters resilience and self-compassion, and empowers others to overcome barriers and truly shine.

Shana is also an avid animal lover and nature nerd. Off-duty, you might find her hiking or kayaking, playing disc golf alongside her husband, caring for her mix of official and unofficial pets, or enjoying a great book or movie.

Connect with Shana at www.ROARify.com.

CHAPTER 15

Unleash the Power of Your Voice: Three Steps to Confidence

Stacey Ellen

This chapter is dedicated to you, dear reader. May you gain insights, knowledge, and inspiration to awaken your voice and the courage you already have within.

Do you ever wonder if you could positively change the world? Or, have you ever felt you had something significant to say but were too nervous to share your voice?

We gain confidence by owning our voice and learning to communicate confidently and speak from our hearts. Then, we gain power by using our voices in the world to effect change.

There are three crucial steps to unleash the power of your voice: build your self-worth, become fully expressed, and then take inspired actions toward your deepest desires.

We've all had to make many choices in life without always knowing the outcome. One of my most significant choices was the decision between becoming an entrepreneur and working for myself or remaining content working for someone else. For many years I worked in corporate sales to increase revenue and bring in more customers, but despite the success I experienced, I never felt fulfilled. In 2008, I was in a sales meeting with my team at the corporation where I worked. One by one, each salesperson took their turn and shared successes and feedback for team productivity. I sat there dreading my turn as I listened to my co-workers speak with ease. Everyone seemed to know exactly what they would say, and it flowed effortlessly from their mouths. As my turn approached, I wanted to run out of the building. I could feel my face turn red and my knees buckling with anticipation as I knew I was about to be called on. I wondered, "Why is it so difficult for me to share? Why do I lose confidence whenever I need to give my opinions, thoughts, and ideas?" I knew I wouldn't have the position if they didn't believe I could do the job and contribute to the company. However, I still lacked the courage to speak confidently in front of my peers.

Has this ever happened to you? You're about to be called on in a group of people, and fear creeps in, so you panic, begin to feel embarrassed, or don't know what to say. Or, maybe you're on stage or in front of a group of people presenting and completely black out or forget what you'll say?

Do not worry; this happens to the best of us. Speaking anxiety or public speaking is listed as one of the top three fears of people today. Glossophobia, the fear of public speaking, is considered one of the most common phobias. Surveys suggest that up to 77% of the population experience some level of anxiety related to public speaking.

So, if you haven't figured out how to effectively use your voice and express yourself, you're not alone. However, it's probably costing you great happiness and income. How you confidently show up in your interactions as an entrepreneur or business professional affects all business areas.

Examples of where you might have trouble using your voice are:

a) If you're afraid to charge what you're worth and charge only what you think a customer might pay, you're not getting paid what you're worth;

b) If you're not making irresistible offers to your ideal clients, you're not making money; or

c) If you're not sharing yourself on social media, making videos, or getting in front of people live; you probably don't have enough of an audience to sell to.

Building your confidence and your voice helps you become known as a leader in your field.

It wasn't long ago that I was in a similar position, not feeling confident or sharing my voice with the world. I've always believed that it was possible for everyone to create a dream life, but I knew I had to take the first step and be an example before I could help others. I had a choice to stay where I was or do something different to get different results. I chose the latter.

I dove deep into personal growth in my early 30s, working with a coach to acknowledge, understand, and change old habits and beliefs. Doing this type of "inner work" on yourself isn't a two-week process. It takes time, dedication, and becoming humble enough to see yourself from the inside out. Was it always easy? No. Did I always enjoy the process? No. However, the outcome far outweighed the difficult times and helped me create the life I love.

As I transformed my inner world, my outer world followed. I got married, had a baby, moved to a dream home, and my business financially exploded. I've spoken around the world for entrepreneurs in businesses, podcasts, summits, and challenges and launched many of my own programs. I've shared stages with many well-known experts, and I'm living my dream of helping others learn to use their voice and passion to build businesses and share their knowledge with the world.

This brings me to you. Do you want to connect to the limitless power that resides within you? If you answered yes, the information below will help you attract more opportunities, gain more business, and use your powerful voice in any situation. Follow these three main strategies, and your world will transform: embrace your self-worth, learn how to express yourself fully, and take inspired actions toward your deepest desires.

First, you must know your self-worth.

The more you believe that everything you have to say is valuable and that you matter, the more outside opinions start to fade. Your confidence soars when you share what's in your heart to help others instead of seeking validation from others.

If you don't currently have everything you desire, you have some resistance or belief in the way of your success. It's your job to uncover where this belief resides, what this belief is, and why you hold some form of subconscious satisfaction to hold onto it.

It can be easy to slide down a negative rabbit hole of thoughts. When you become present and acknowledge your thoughts moment-by-moment, you can catch yourself and redirect the thought with a more positive one. One practice I teach my clients to become more present is to clear their thoughts and focus on something in front of them while softening their eyes. Take three slow, deep breaths, counting to five on the inhale through the nose, then five on the exhale through the mouth, only focusing on the sound of your breath. This quick practice will immediately shift your energy and take you out of the negative thought patterns and into a more relaxed state.

My client Bill noticed an immediate shift in his fearful energy when he was about to speak in front of a crowd. He saw his negative thoughts and began to take some deep, slow breaths to calm his nervous system. He shared how quickly he noticed his breath practices calmed his nerves and gave him the confidence to tune back into his heart. His calm confidence helped his message be clear and concise when he spoke. He connected to the crowd with his energy, and his message and stories made his talk exciting and memorable. He wasn't projecting and teaching "at" people anymore; he was connecting with them on a heart level. At the end of his talk, he made a sales offer and was shocked at how many people signed up to work with him. Bill gained great insight and confidence using these techniques, and as a result, his message was well-received and profitable for himself and others.

Another practice that can build confidence and awareness is meditation. Creating quiet time for yourself is one of the best practices with multiple physical, mental, and emotional benefits. Now, hear me out. You don't need to sit for hours wrestling with your mind and making 'ohm noises.' Walking outside without a device in hand and getting present to the environment while embracing all its beauty is also a form of meditation. As mentioned above, you can start by breathing and clearing your mind and thoughts of all distractions. What my clients and I've found that often helps is listening to guided meditation and following along. If this feels more your speed, go here to download a free, quick 10-minute meditation I created to help relieve any anxiety in less than 10 minutes https://go.staceyellen. com/meditation.

*The next step to building confidence is to become fully
expressed as an individual. Being fully expressed takes
courage, and courage creates confidence.*

"How does one do this," I often get asked.

You get to practice loving and embracing all you are to fully embody your best qualities and share them with the world. You were born with specific strengths, talents, and attributes no one else has. Sharing your gifts with the world helps you come out of your shell and own your authentic self. In turn, you will attract the right people into your space, and others will benefit from your self-expression. People will be drawn to your bravery, your knowledge, and your confidence will shine through your energy.

We all tend to be fearful prisoners of our own perceived limitations. When you stop thinking you can't do something and embrace your talents and strengths, you positively redirect your energy. Delete the word "can't" from your vocabulary because words are powerful; then notice how you will immediately think about why you "can" do something. Our language is tied to our thoughts, so change your language, and your confident thoughts will follow suit.

Courage and perseverance are needed for personal growth. I used to be on a speaking circuit where we visited different cities and spoke to different crowds of business owners and entrepreneurs. We were in Texas, and it was my turn to speak in front of hundreds of people. In the middle of my talk, I started to feel like I was about to pass out and had to leave the room. To make matters worse, the event's founder wasn't keen on speakers not finishing their talks, so I didn't think I'd be asked back. Needless to say, my confidence was shaken. A few hours later, I felt back to myself and thought that if I didn't ask to finish my talk, I would regret it. I owed it to the audience to finish my story, even if it made a difference in just one person's life that day. To my surprise, the audience clapped and welcomed me back with open arms. I joked, "Now I'm ready and pleased to see you all again," and they all smiled. Several people even signed up to work with me that day. Additionally, a few more seasoned speakers even told me I was now an official "seasoned speaker" because everyone falls at least once in their career.

Perseverance in the face of adversity is what builds character and confidence. When you do the thing you fear the most, you gain courage. Our confidence grows by bouncing back from setbacks and trying again, even after "we think" we have failed. We learn more from our setbacks and failures than from our victories. Sometimes, a slight tweak in your thoughts and actions is needed to move toward your desired goals, and the day I left the stage helped me stop worrying about what others were thinking and stand powerfully in my energy. Comparison is always the thief of joy and self-confidence. I got to see firsthand that people wanted to hear my story. My message needed to be heard, and so does yours.

The more you share your thoughts, beliefs, knowledge, and values, the more you attract people with similar belief systems. People relate to authenticity and your ability to share even when you have an unpopular opinion or share your vulnerability. You have your unique way of talking, sharing, advising, and teaching that no one else can replicate. If you remain consistent in sharing your expertise with authenticity, you will begin to position yourself as a confident go-to resource and a thought leader in your field.

People will relate to you when you share your stories and experiences. They don't want to hear the same strategies others teach; they want to listen to what you and your clients have gone through to achieve their goals. This may feel unsafe at first, but the more you practice, the easier it will become to confidently share more about yourself and your experiences.

If you want to conquer your speaking fears and transform anxiety into powerful confidence, I have another free resource for you. Check out this video to eliminate speaking anxiety with these five steps! Go to https://go.staceyellen.com/speaking-fears.

The third step is to take inspired action
toward your dreams.

When we are confident in what we offer in any business, it is easy to see the value of our services and ask for what we are worth. Our personal comfort zone often keeps us locked away from our greatest ideas, opportunities, and most confident selves.

Taking inspired action is when you allow yourself to have boundaries and say yes to things aligned with your current goals, then filter out everything else. When you learn to tune into your intuition, you will feel what is in your highest good to act upon in each moment. If you jump at all opportunities, your energies will scatter, and your message can get watered down. Alternatively, opportunities can pass you by if you don't follow those inner nudges. Taking inspired action will help you gain courage and learn every step of the way.

My client Kristi had worked with other coaches but wasn't seeing the progress she wanted to see in her business and desperately wanted things to change. She trusted her intuition and said yes to working together even though the investment took her out of her comfort zone. Kristi was tired of trading time for money and began to resent her business as she lived in scarcity. After doing some deep inner work, she took ownership of her emotions, attitude, and responsibility for her actions. Our work together helped her begin to heal from the inside/out. She began to trust herself and her choices, which led to more self-confidence. Her business exploded as she shifted from hating sales to being comfortable serving others. When Kristi spoke from her heart, she quickly connected with clients, which helped increase her sales. Her revenue began to explode from 2K to

13K months, allowing her to pay off her credit cards and hire her first assistant. The best part is that she now enjoys having her own business again.

Kristi is an amazing example of how building self-confidence and self-worth is directly related to your business success. You see, the energy you put into the world is always attracting people to you or repelling people from you. When you say yes to yourself and begin to do the inner work alongside creating new business strategies, everything will transform around you.

We always get nudges, ideas, or sensations about the next best move. It's our job to get out of our way and focus back on our heart and inner guidance system (IGS) to hear the guidance. From here, it's much easier to take inspired action on the guidance and watch as more aligned opportunities unfold. We all have a certain amount of time on this planet, and what we do with that time determines how fulfilled we are here. Building more confidence helps us find that inner peace and joy we crave.

Your life will transform if you follow these three main strategies: embrace your self-worth, become fully expressed and take inspired actions toward your deepest desires.

Building your self-confidence empowers you as an individual. Sharing your fullest expression connects you with others and helps build long-lasting relationships. Then, taking inspired, actionable steps forward puts you center stage to obtain all you desire in life.

You now have a choice. I invite you to look at your life and your business and notice if there is anything you want to shift or change. Do you have the income you desire? Are you sharing your message with audiences around the world? Are you helping the amount of people you wish to serve? Or do you know there's more you want to accomplish?

We don't always know how to create or welcome change in our lives. As Les Brown says, "We can't see the forest through the trees." Acknowledging what's not working is always the first step toward creating change. Having a coach as an impartial support system that listens and supports without judgment was the number one thing that helped me build confidence and create my dream life.

Many clients I've worked with have increased their income, gained speaking opportunities, learned how to position themselves in a saturated marketplace, and felt more confident in every area of their lives. When you take the time to transform one area of your life, many other areas are positively affected. If you would like help along your journey, I would be honored to be your support system. You can find out more information at www.staceyellen.com. Whether we get to know each other or not, I appreciate your openness to explore options to transform your life. And now that you've had a breakthrough, the choice is always yours; what do you do next? I'm excited to see what you create!

To your success, Stacey

Stacey Ellen

Stacey Ellen guides business entrepreneurs and leaders who want to become better speakers, create sales, gain confidence, and live abundant lives. With over two decades of business experience, Stacey's passion is guiding business owners to uplevel their mindset and energy, own their voice, and use heart-based business strategies.

She is a Business Coach, Author, Speaker, and CEO of RebelHeart Leaders, a business and life mentoring company. Passionate about business and personal growth, Stacey has worked with some top experts while helping hundreds of people worldwide learn their recipe for business success and individual achievements.

Audiences who hear her speak love her heart-centered approach to training and gain knowledge they can implement quickly to get results in their business and life. Stacey has shared stages with many well-known experts worldwide while guiding people to move through obstacles, stand firm in their power, and lead with heart.

She has contributed to three best-selling books, and her clients often call her their "secret weapon" as she guides them to become the best version of themselves and connect to the abundance around them.

Stacey currently lives in Colorado with her husband, son, and two cats, and in her free time, she enjoys hiking and anything revolving around music.

To learn more, visit www.staceyellen.com.

CHAPTER 16

All Is Sinking Sand...or Is It?

Stephanie Myers

This chapter is dedicated to my mother, Mary Myers. She
fought the good fight of faith and won.
I miss you, Mommy.

Wow! This life is so full of twists and turns, ups and downs that it can be daunting to keep one's confidence level up...let alone HIGH! The best of us find this a challenge, so how does a person like me (or should I say, how I used to be) choose confidence when every bone in your body senses that life will never get better? What do you do when all is sinking sand?

Confidence can be slippery. The word I really want to use is tricky but that depends on the individual. When our lives are pleasant and life puts a smile on our faces, then we deem life as good and our confidence level can maintain itself. We can manage this level of confidence because we are comfortable. Since nothing in our life has taken a sharp turn for the worse, we often take on the outlook that things can only get better. Our confidence can grow higher and higher and higher. Let your dreams soar (have you heard that before)! I suppose if you had a decent to good childhood, you could gauge confidence on that scale and possibly continue using that same gauge throughout your life. But what if your childhood was not so great? The lens of life reveals a chasm in thinking that can point downward and instead of seeing sunshine all that person may see is the hard ground of disappointment and neglect. The foundation we build our confidence on from childhood is vitally important and not to be underestimated.

Chapter One: Everyone Else Is Doing It

If we are honest, thinking back to our teenage years, we have always wanted to do what "everyone else was doing." The more fun that everyone else was having made us want to join in. Do you remember those days? It's called inclusion. We all want to be included in something. That way we are not alone. From a confidence perspective, as long as we are not alone and others are involved and happy, we can be involved and happy, too. There is something to be noted about happiness and confidence. The shift in confidence comes when there is no inclusion and a person believes he or she is left alone to sink.

Imagine being out for a walk near the coastline or riverbank when you step into quicksand. If panic sets in quickly (ah, yeah), chances of you escaping are slim. By that same analogy, when our confidence level takes a hit and something goes wrong and cannot be corrected in minutes, the confidence that we once held onto can leave us feeling alone and isolated even when in a crowd of people. The last thing anyone should do is withdraw. Instead, seek friends and family that you trust and talk (not argue) about what concerns you. Notice I stated "trust." If you do not have someone you trust, then do not allow your confidence to further sink but reach out to a professional.

Speaking with someone who has your best interest at heart and no connection to the source of your problem can be refreshing. You can be yourself without feeling the need to hide or pretend to make things appear better than they are. This support, either from friends and family or a professional, can be like a lifeline thrown out to you when you are sinking. Additionally, you are not alone. You have support which is essential to maintaining a healthy confidence level. So many people in the world say that talk is cheap but when you need a lifeline, talking things through can open your perspective and have you look at that same situation in a better light. You are pulled out of the quicksand and can feel the sunshine on your face. That feels good, right? Remember, for some of us it is not about an overabundance of confidence. It is more about maintaining a healthy confidence level. You are choosing confidence. Doing what everyone else is doing, thinking like everyone else is thinking can be tricky because those ways may not align with the person you are. Being true to yourself adds to your confidence level. Build your foundation on that.

Chapter 2: Life Is Just Too Hard

Hey, I get it. Life is hard for many people and appears to only be getting harder. It is easy to see people who have more than us and believe they live a less complicated life because of the monetary status they have accrued or inherited. I'll be the first to admit that money makes life easier in so many ways. But don't be fooled. Money doesn't solve everything. Your happiness and your confidence should not depend on the amount of coins you have.

Think back to a time when you were happy or near happy. When was the last time you remembered that moment in time? So many people center their thoughts on the negative episodes in life instead of focusing on the times that did make them smile. Are you one of those people? Let me tell you my own experience.

It is easy for me to look at the negative side of everything and allow those thoughts to take over my entire thinking process. I would look for the negative and then have my thought processes expand upon it.

This made the situation so much worse than it was. I had been doing this for so long that I didn't even realize this was a button that was always "on" in my mind. Sure, life throws us into pitfalls, but what are we doing to get ourselves back out? I grew tired of coming from a defeatist mentality all the time. I wanted to win. This meant I had to change the way I was thinking (all is sinking sand) and shift my mind to a better place...the place where I am the survivor of my negativity.

I am not suggesting that you do not own what has happened to you. Not replacing reality for fantasy. I'm saying that no matter what my experience is, I was not going to swim in the pool of despair and allow that to shape my viewpoint on life. When you do that, the negativity spreads and it can be very difficult to get your mind out of that type of thinking.

Riches cannot save you. You have to save yourself and you do this by finding the good out of the bad. Finding the good out of the bad? What does that mean? That means taking the bad experience that you went through and being thankful that you made it out...you made it through. This is where gratefulness comes into play.

It is imperative that you realize you survived and made it out when others didn't. That in itself can make you feel better about life because you get another chance for the goodness that life is offering. Your confidence has a chance to grow higher, deeper, and wider! Being grateful is a key gateway to confidence building. When you are grateful for what you have experienced and made it through that ordeal, you can see its beauty. Now you can shape that experience to best suit you and what you need. You control your mind. You choose confidence and you build upon the positive aspect. One aspect is that you did not allow the experience to wipe you out. You have something left over and with the right mindset, you are choosing confidence instead of defeat.

Money and the riches of this world will not prevent your mind from being attacked with feelings of despair and hopelessness. Advice from social media sites will not help you. Frustration, when not addressed properly, can easily turn into despair, bitterness, and anger. Please do not allow those feelings to grow. Decide today to choose confidence and take the necessary steps to help yourself to heal. Follow along and learn how to help yourself to see a brighter day. Depending on where your mind is now, this day is not far off.

Chapter 3: Comfort in Our Thoughts

This may be hard to believe, but some people take comfort in having feelings and thoughts of despair. Beliefs and feelings of "life owes me something" or "this happened to me so I cannot be expected to shine brightly" are just a few of the excuses used by those who have given up on seeking a brighter light... a better day. Do not let this be you.

The experiences of my own life could have sent me on a journey filled with self-hate and self-loathing. There were times I couldn't see (or chose not to see) a way to have a better day. I would stay stuck in my mind...a room filled with darkness. There was a comfort in just knowing that nothing was expected of me but to sulk about my situation. There was no need to gather the courage to improve things. Nothing within me sensed that a better day was even possible, plus I could gain pity from others if they knew of my circumstances. There was no accountability...not even to myself.

It can become so easy to stay in the state of mind. I lacked the confidence to cheer myself on to a better day. Every day was just a sad state of affairs. I told myself that life offered me nothing and that life had nothing good in store for me. I was young and had those thoughts! Having someone with whom you trust is essential to break the spirit of despair that hangs out and lives with you. Talking to someone near and dear who believes in you and can counsel you to look at your situation in a more positive light is crucial to your well-being. You may be unable to do this yourself because as soon as you have a glimpse of the positive, the majority of your thinking, being negative, will swallow up any good that comes to your mind. You will need support. A listening friend, family member, or professional therapist who can help you along your journey to see a better day ahead is a gratefulness that cannot be measured.

Chapter 4: Yes, I'm a People-Pleaser

I have always wanted to be liked, if not loved, by everyone. I wanted people to be happy with me. I wanted folks to speak highly of me when I was around and even if I was not around. My strategy? Just do as everyone wants and tell nobody "No." That was the plan. I knew that as long as people were pleased with me helping them, I would always receive great compliments about being such a good woman. I never anticipated the costs...the toll all this people-pleasing would eventually have on my mind, body, and spirit.

I remember my mother always saying that life is ultimately about our choices. I never chose confidence because I always chose people-pleasing. I figured that that was enough as long as the people were pleased (parents, church, work, neighbors, friends). Boy, was I wrong!

It was a work experience that made me say "no" first. I had work that had to be completed before I left for the weekend with my boyfriend. I was almost finished when a coworker was having trouble completing their job assignment. Normally, I help others when needed and vice versa. This individual I have helped numerous times in the past. I don't try to hold it against anyone if they stay a little too long at lunch or keep taking numerous breaks when on a deadline. I still try and help out. Until the day that I wanted to leave work on time because it was Fourth of July weekend and I was looking forward to a long-overdue weekend with my special friend. It was almost time to go when *%$#! My coworker comes in 30 minutes before time to leave work asking for help. I looked at the clock even though I knew exactly what time it was. I said, "No, I'm leaving on time today." Helping out would take at least 45 minutes to an hour, with me doing most of the work (past experience with this particular individual). It did not go well. My coworker was expecting me to say "yes" as always. In fact, she waited for me to repeat it to make certain she heard me correctly the first time. Needless to say, once I returned to work, my reputation had taken a hit. I was no longer the person willing to help everyone out. Now, I was the person who didn't help a coworker because I was a selfish individual who only thought of herself.

Lesson: You will never build your confidence if you depend on other people to keep lifting you. As soon as you make a decision that goes contrary to what they expect of you, the shakedown begins. Yes, I could have worked over (no fun) or just left with no regrets (fun). I did not get down on myself either. I kept my confidence despite not pleasing this particular person. I think it was because I have helped them so many times in the past that I did not regret not helping out this one time. I hated that they turned on me but that also showed me they were not a friend. I was just being used for their agenda. From that day forward, I have built upon my confidence. All is not sinking sand. Sometimes, all is a solid foundation on which to build.

Chapter 5: My Foundation

I wish I could write this chapter and tell you that all it took for me to build upon my confidence was to make smart choices. That would be a lie. I have made many wrong moves and taken many wrong turns in my life. I have been brought low just to pick myself up and strive to go higher, if only an inch higher than where I was before. My foundation I ultimately realized after much trial and error was built on Jesus Christ. See, I had gotten so low on myself that I had nowhere else to turn but Christ. His Holiness saw the beauty inside of me. Now, I am not here to preach to anyone because I know all people have not the faith. I just did not want you to think that everything regarding the high self-confidence that I now hold within myself was due to my know-how and skill. Left to my own devices, I would have gone down in quicksand.

There came a time when good friends and a great therapist still left me empty and incomplete. I needed a spiritual connection to my Creator. Christ is what lifted my head and made me take notice of the warmth of the sun and the beautiful life that was ahead of me. He took away the negative thoughts and brought me into His glorious Light.

What I will say is that I hope you have a real support network when your life crashes against the rocks. Some people's bad times hit harder than others but one thing is for sure: We all need a great pick-me-up sooner rather than later. I pray you have that because your confidence should be built on a sure foundation. One that will not change with the wind or expect more than you are ready to give. A foundation that does not take but freely gives to you. More importantly, does so without condemning you for giving nothing back in return. This is where being thankful for your life (because it can get better) and being grateful for where you are now (because your confidence can grow and deepen). These are two great options to have in life. I hope you realize this. In a world where many are losing hope, your confidence is a stabilizer against pessimism. You will need that stabilizer, trust me.

Chapter 6: Confidence Builders

There are some tips that I have found to be useful in building my confidence. I would like to share them with you in the hope that these will help you to become more self-aware about how you are feeling and not go out on a downward spiral attacking yourself. I am a confidence builder, not a confidence killer.

Affirmations: I have always looked for positive affirmations or quotes that resonated with my soul and spoke to my spirit. This helped to brighten my day a little bit.

I sought a support network: I had one person that I counted on and trusted they had my best intentions at heart. It helped me to spill my guts to her without fear of judgment.

Time out for negative thoughts: I languished in negative thoughts all day every day. Do not do this! It's a trap to keep your mind in a defeated position so you never build your confidence toward anything.

I opened myself up to new experiences: Namely, I tried yoga and deep breathing exercises. At first, I refused to go to yoga or even try Square breathing, but I decided if things were going to change, I had to be the one to change them. Doing the same old thing was getting me nowhere.

Be Thankful: I realized that being thankful for what I endured throughout my life has only made me a better person, not a weaker one. I am stronger today because I survived and my confidence reflects that.

Stephanie Myers

Stephanie Myers is a seasoned advocate and change-maker with over two decades of experience in male-dominated industries. Raised in an environment that often relegated women to second-class status, Stephanie was inspired by her mother, Mary, a resolute and competent woman who taught her to value her own strengths and individuality beyond societal expectations. This foundational belief fueled Stephanie's determination to alter the narrative for herself and other women striving to make their mark.

As an advocate for gender equity globally, Stephanie believes that exposing and challenging the biases women face is essential to the fight for gender equality. Her work serves as both a testimony and a guide, helping others recognize that women are capable of achieving anything they set their minds to and should be afforded the same privileges—recognition, compensation, and opportunities—that their male counterparts often receive.

Connect with Stephanie at

https://www.biasbreakingbeauty.com.

CHAPTER 17

The Audacity to Choose Confidence

Stephanie Young

This chapter is dedicated to my husband Jon and son Owen who give the best "mommy sandwich" hugs!

It may shock people who know me, but at age 13 I didn't want to be alive anymore. So much so that I attempted to make that happen twice.

The second time, I remember sitting on my bed, completely unable to move, but begging God to let me wake up in the morning.

Confidence as a 13-year-old felt hard to come by.

But I had no clue what was going to happen later that year to set me on a path to where I am now.

There were twists and turns. Definitely days when I wondered if it would have been better had my plan worked and I'd not woken up.

I am so relieved and grateful now, in my late 30s, that I'm here.

As I navigated my journey, I realized that confidence is not just a feeling that magically appears; it's a choice. It requires audacity, especially when life throws unexpected challenges our way. This brings me to an essential aspect of my growth that I discovered along my journey.

The Audacity to Choose Confidence

It took me years to recognize a correlation between organization and confidence. Bonkers, right? But it's true.

I was a disorganized mess, not getting things done, feeling like crap, and wondering if something was wrong with me.

After learning in college that I have ADHD, things started making sense. My brain works differently, beautifully. It simply needed different tools to work. Having spent 20+ years not having the correct tools, my confidence felt fake and it often was.

Finally, I found tools to help me stay organized. In my organization, I felt amazing! Things were falling through the cracks infrequently. I plan my life around my goals. And I started to see more success in my life.

Discovering Leadership Through Organization

At 13, after surviving my suicide attempts and deciding to LIVE, I was asked to teach middle schoolers from our youth group to go into inner-city Baltimore to support a thriving ministry—this involved planning lessons, coordinating volunteers, and managing logistics. Parents often questioned why someone so young was in charge, doubting my ability to provide the necessary information and teach effectively.

The first trip was successful and I was asked back as the middle school leader four more times, creating many fun memories with the students and learning some valuable lessons on confident leadership.

When I was asked to join the Taste of Missions committee at 16, I was younger than the rest by at least 15 years. They wanted me to recruit 75 teenagers for various roles at our missions conference. They even said, "We'll be happy with 50. Teenagers are unreliable."

Determined to prove them wrong, I recruited 110, and 109 showed up. Managing these volunteers required coordinating via email and text and keeping all the assignments in a spreadsheet. I was asked back the second year, and once again, we had a 99% show up rate.

High school was a period of significant growth and responsibility. As class president, I managed meetings, planned events, and coordinated with students and faculty. Plus helping plan and execute the fundraising for our senior class trip was a significant responsibility. We enjoyed an amazing week in Costa Rica!

Managing deadlines and coordinating with team members as the yearbook editor also required strong organizational skills. It was sometimes challenging to be in charge of my peers, as it is much easier for teenagers to respect an adult than someone their own age.

My role as yearbook editor required meticulous planning and attention to detail, ensuring that deadlines were met and that the final product was something we could all be proud of.

Overcoming Setbacks: Staying Organized and Resilient

College presented significant challenges, including failing crucial classes that caused me to change my major. I'd thought that I wanted to be a youth pastor with a counseling degree. After failing one of the required courses for each degree, I discovered that dream was not truly what I wanted. Switching my major to Business Management was one of the smartest decisions I made. I thrived in those courses, completely falling in love with the aspects of running a business.

College Struggles

College was rough at first. I felt lonely and very much a fish out of water. I went from being known to being completely unknown, which shook me! I thought college wasn't right for me. Maybe I wasn't meant to be a leader at all. I struggled with having to set my schedule for classes and studying. Even though I bought a ton of planners, folders, binders, and highlighters, it was a struggle. This is when I learned that I had ADHD and things started making sense. Traditional organizational and study tricks didn't work for me. I needed something different. Learning how to organize in a way my brain liked brought tremendous confidence.

Job Losses

I've lost a handful of jobs over the years, often due to my ability to let my ADHD run wild rather than using the tools that work for me.

The job loss that shook me the most was one I had wanted for years.

I'd applied to the company five times for five different positions. The job I finally interviewed for differed from the one I was offered. I was told I was the second choice, but someone on the interview panel had been very impressed with how prepared I was. They remarked that this was the first time anyone made a folder with labeled tabs for things they might want to review in the interview.

Though sad about how that position ended, it set me on a path to where I am now. Because of that job loss and my husband's encouragement, I started selling LuLaRoe (a direct sales clothing line) full time. I joined Molly Mahoney's GLAM (Go Live And Monetize) program to take my business to the next level. In her program, I found the confidence to start my own coaching business, helping others get organized using the tools I'd learned over the past few years. (My favorite tool is Google Suite, in case you were wondering.)

Role Models and Inspirations: Learning Organizational Skills

For five years, I competed in a Fine Arts Festival that my church participated in. Every year I made it from the district level to the national level. It's something I'm still proud of.

Marc and Cyndi have been involved in my life since childhood. They encouraged me in the kids' choir, though I wasn't a strong singer.

They recommended me to be the middle school missions leader and the Taste of Missions Youth liaison that I mentioned previously. They encouraged me when I competed in Fine Arts, and were on many missions trips that I participated in.

After I got married, they encouraged and mentored us. When we needed recommendation letters for our adoption, they were the first couple we thought of. Before we adopted, we saw how they interacted with their kids and agreed that we wanted to model our parenting after them.

Gary and Collette were very present in my teen years. They typically mentored the singing students. I was NOT a singer. And there wasn't a huge reason for them to take an interest in my categories, but they did. Both of them poured love and encouragement into me from 8th grade to my senior year, constantly cheering me on.

In my fifth year of competition and senior year of high school, I felt like I needed to be more confident about a few categories I'd chosen to compete in. They both encouraged me leading up to the district level of competition. Gary even said, "We never doubted you'd advance to nationals." That has stuck with me for years, that the mentors in my life did not doubt my ability to succeed.

Personal Growth and Development: Enhancing Organizational Skills

Personal growth has been a cornerstone of my confidence. As a leadership minor in college, I participated in mentoring teams, student council, and new student orientation.

College and Professional Development

In college, I felt incredibly lonely during my freshman year. So much so that I signed up to help with new student orientation so I could meet people my sophomore year. I also decided that the very first opportunity that was presented to me to join a club, team, or committee, I would do it. Enter the force of nature, Krissi. She was everything I wanted to be: bold, witty, fabulous! She was our class president for three years, and I was her secretary all three years. Together, we planned fundraisers, banquets, and more. Her courage to be herself pushed me to find the same courage within. I'll always be grateful for her friendship and how she impacted me. She's a writer now, and it's a joy to read her writing, knowing she's living her dream!

Working With Molly Mahoney

After being in the GLAM program for 1.5 years, I realized that someday I would like to be on Molly's team if the correct position and timing lined up. We discussed it every time we saw each other, and I did everything possible to attend any event she hosted because I knew that being in proximity to what I wanted would help!

And boy, did it!

In June of 2023, Molly offered me the position of Executive Assistant. I accepted and have celebrated one year on the Prepared Performer Team as of the publishing of this book.

I could make the thing I wanted come to fruition through patience, persistence, and proximity. This also required me to be audacious when asking for what I wanted. Audacity can be and is a beautiful thing. It's what I call my confidence!

Impact on Life and Work: Organization in Action

My confidence has significantly influenced my career at The Prepared Performer. Transitioning from a client to the Executive Assistant and eventually becoming Chief of Staff was possible because of my organizational skills.

Personal Relationships

My organizational skills have positively affected my relationships with friends, family, and colleagues. For example, planning family events, coordinating schedules with friends, and managing work-life balance all benefit from solid organizational habits.

Practical Tips

The most important lessons I've learned about confidence and organization include being patient with yourself, persistent in your efforts, and proactive in your environment. If you are looking to improve your organizational skills, here are some practical tips:

- **Set Clear Goals**: Define what you want to achieve and break it down into manageable steps.
    - Saying "I want to go to Tokyo" sounds great on a list, but a clear goal breaks that down into actionable steps.
        - Do I have a valid passport?
        - Do I have the ability to take time off of work?
        - How much are the plane tickets and do I need to save for them?
        - Where do I want to stay in Tokyo?
        - What do I want to see and experience while there?
- **Start Small**: Begin with organizing one area of your life, whether it's your workspace, schedule, or a specific project.
    - Consider what's involved in decluttering a room.
        - First, remove the trash. It's easier to work in a cleaner environment.

- Second, remove the items that you know do not live in that space.
  - i.e., if you're decluttering the living room, dishes need to go back to the kitchen.
    - Third, sort items that do need to stay in the space.
    - Fourth, give the items that stay a home.
      - Pillows on the couch.
      - Remote on the side or coffee table.
      - Toys in the bin or on shelves.
    - Fifth, if you have items that do not yet have a home and don't have the energy to sort them, simply place them in a box and select a date to sort later, then put that date on your calendar so you don't forget.
- **Use Tools**: Utilize planners, apps, and other organizational tools to keep track of tasks and deadlines.
  - As a planner addict, I can safely say that there is no one perfect planner.
    - Find the brand that works for you and use it. I'm a fan of the ...
      - Day Designer which can be found at Target or online. Their month/day planner is simple and easy to use.
      - If you want something fancier, The Passion Planner and Golden Coil are fantastic!
      - Consider going digital as many calendars are free, like my favorite calendar, Google!
      - The joy of Google is that you can use the calendar with their other products, thereby keeping things cohesive.

- **Stay Consistent**: Regularly review and adjust your plans to stay on track.
  - o Set a date with yourself monthly, or weekly if you are able, to review your goals and tools.
    - Are the tools working for what you need?
    - Are the goals realistic and achievable?
    - Have you created time in your calendar to work on the goals?

Embracing an Organized Life

Reflecting on my journey, I realize that being organized has been a fundamental part of my confidence. Each organized step has led to more extraordinary achievements and a stronger belief in my capabilities. Today, I am proud of where I am and excited about future possibilities.

Deep Reflection

When people ask me how I got where I am, I often tell them:

1. **Audacity**: Being bold and choosing confidence.
2. **Persistence**: Continuing to ask for what I want, sharing what I want, and not letting setbacks stop me.
3. **Patience**: Not giving up when things don't work out the first time. If they're right, they will work out.
4. **Proximity**: Being near the thing I want! If you want to be organized, spend time with people who are organized. These principles have guided my journey and helped me build a life filled with purpose and confidence.

Future Goals

My whole goal in life is to help others. I feel like I would be remiss if I didn't share with you my goals. I aspire to:

- <u>Speak on Stages with Molly</u>: I want to share our journey and strategies for achieving life goals with a broader audience.
- <u>Write Children's Books</u>: I dream of writing books on confidence, strength, and kindness, aiming to inspire the next generation.
- <u>Support Others</u>: I want to be known as a woman who supports others in achieving what they want in life—a helper.

Being part of The Prepared Performer team has been an incredible journey. It's a privilege to work alongside such dedicated and talented individuals. My boss, Molly Mahoney, who is also involved in this book, has been a tremendous influence and support.

The Audacity to Choose Confidence

In conclusion, the audacity to choose confidence is about believing in yourself and being organized and prepared to face any challenge. My journey from a disorganized mess to a confident, organized leader is a testament to the power of organization in building confidence. By staying organized, being persistent and patient, and placing yourself in proximity to your goals, you, too, can achieve the confidence and success you desire.

Confidence is a journey, not a destination. Embrace your unique path, find the tools that work for you, and never be afraid to be audaciously confident.

Stephanie Young

Stephanie Young is the Chief of Staff at The Prepared Performer, where she brings her extensive experience in management and organizational leadership to support the team and clients. With a BS in Business Management and a minor in Leadership, Stephanie's diverse professional background includes roles as a manager at Chipotle and Things Remembered, a Lab Coordinator at a research facility, a leasing associate, a LuLaRoe consultant, and customer service at a car dealership.

Stephanie is known for her exceptional organizational skills, confidence, and leadership qualities. Her journey through various industries has equipped her with a unique perspective and a versatile skillset. Joining Molly Mahoney's team has been a highlight of her career, where she takes pride in contributing to the company's mission and success.

In addition to her professional achievements, Stephanie is passionate about personal growth and development. She loves to read, bake, and is currently learning to sew. Stephanie's dedication to helping others achieve their goals and her commitment to continuous improvement make her a valued member of The Prepared Performer team.

Connect with Stephanie at

www.ThePreparedPerformer.com.

CHAPTER 18

Finding Hope: Tracy's Journey from Despair to Empowerment

Tracy Weskamp

To my beautiful daughters, Anna and Catherine – You are my greatest joy and inspiration. This story is for you, a testament to the human spirit's potential. Your unwavering belief in me has fueled my journey. May it remind you that with love, belief, and tenacity, anything is possible. All my love, Mom

---

Courage and confidence are the twin pillars that support any significant life change. They empower us to step out of our comfort zone and into the unknown, transforming fear into action and dreams into reality. I want to share how digging deep to embrace these qualities guided me through one of the most pivotal transitions in my life: leaving a successful corporate career to follow my passion for natural health and success coaching.

I remember the days when I felt like many of you—exhausted, overwhelmed, and trapped in a body that no longer felt like mine. I was the Global Vice President of Consumer Research & Product Development for a billion-dollar company, leading a high-stakes career that demanded every ounce of my energy and focus. I was also a single parent to my beautiful twin daughters. To put it simply, I was juggling chainsaws. I loved my family, my job, and the people I worked with, but behind the scenes, I was absolutely crumbling.

A few years prior, at the age of 32, just 14 months after my twin girls were born, I was diagnosed with Young-Onset Parkinson's Disease. The diagnosis came with terrifying predictions from top neurologists: progressive degeneration, inevitable institutionalization, and a radically shortened lifespan. I had watched my grandmother become systematically dismantled and eventually pass away from Parkinson's, so I had a deep understanding of what lay ahead for me. My life, filled with ambition and high achievement, seemed to crumble. I felt like a shadow of the fierce, unstoppable woman I once was, and the weight of that loss was unbearable. I sunk into depression as my health and life began to unravel completely, my once fierce and unstoppable spirit shattered.

I felt helpless as my symptoms worsened despite extensive pharmaceutical therapies. The tremors and falls, the fatigue, the brain fog—they took over my life. I became a shell of the woman who once crushed deadlines and easily navigated boardrooms. I lived my life trying to hide my symptoms from my colleagues, finding any excuse to avoid writing on whiteboards and avoiding laser pointers, both of which put my tremors on full display. As predicted by my doctors, my marriage failed spectacularly, and I was left to raise and support my girls on my own. One winter morning, as I lay at the base of my driveway after yet another fall, I sat in the snow crying, unable to fathom how I would continue. I was dying a slow, miserable death, and I felt powerless to stop it.

Then came a moment that changed everything. One afternoon, as I sat sulking in a heap of self-pity, my sweet little girls crawled into my lap. One looked up at me with innocent eyes and asked, "Mommy, who is going to take care of us when you die?"

Oh, my Lord, those words hit me like a ton of bricks. I realized that I had to snap out of it! I couldn't accept that my body was destined to fall apart, and I certainly couldn't leave my daughters without a mother. In that instant, overcoming this disease became not only possible but a non-negotiable for me. I WOULD get better; I had no doubt. The mindset change was sudden, swift, and critical to my success.

At that time, it wasn't possible to jump on the internet and purchase a "done for you" detox program or to obtain information about how I ended up this sick at such a young age. So, I turned to the library and devoured everything I could about Parkinson's Disease and its suspected root causes. I discovered the strong connection between pesticide exposure and the disease, as well as the benefits of movement. I changed everything about how I lived my life. I began a relentless campaign of the cleanest eating, walking, detoxing, and praying. Slowly, bit by bit, I would reclaim my health, defying the doctors who had written my premature obituary. This was not a quick-fix situation; no magical herbs or instant cures existed.

My journey was filled with setbacks and small victories, and I am grateful for every one of them. After ten years of hard work and unwavering determination, I walked into my neurologist's office, where he finally declared me "symptom-free." He was astonished, and I was thrilled, having maintained my confidence that it was only a matter of time before I was "better."

Today, at 54, I am not just alive; I am thriving. I am a competitive runner, ride horses, and embrace every day with the vitality and energy of someone much younger. My body did not fall apart on me, and yours doesn't have to either. We are meant to live vibrant, energetic, active lives well into our 80s and 90s, and I intend to do precisely that.

The journey to reclaim my health transformed everything about my life and purpose. I was able to experience firsthand the body's incredible ability to heal when toxicities are removed and deficiencies are replaced. I felt a profound calling to support other women who were likely making some of the same mistakes that I had made. After all, I had always been a hard-driving, health-minded person and an athlete for most of my life. Suppose I thought I was doing all of the "right things," and my health nearly evaporated. How many other women were unknowingly poisoning themselves and their families? I eventually came to view my diagnosis as a gift rather than a curse.

As I grew healthier and stronger, I knew that God had given me this "gift" so that I could help others. I left my comfortable corporate role, returned to school, and eventually launched my Integrative Health practice to help hard-driving women entrepreneurs reclaim their health, energy, and confidence. My mission is to guide women to live their most vibrant, thriving lives, free from the constraints of poor health.

Today, I dedicate my life to helping women like you. I know the pain of feeling exhausted, overweight, and brain-fogged. I know what it is like to lose the warrior spirit that once defined you. But I also know the incredible power of the human body to heal itself when given the right tools and support.

It took all the courage I could muster to step into this new role as an Integrative Health Practitioner. I had to harness every ounce of bravery to leave behind the security and prestige of a corporate career and venture into the unknown. The rewards have been immeasurable. I've helped countless women reconnect with their lost mojo, lose stubborn weight, and achieve unparalleled success in all facets of their lives. When your body is thriving, it impacts every aspect of your life most positively!

Finding the Courage to Break Away

I'd like to share a few top tips that enabled me to dig deep and find the courage to make this significant life change.

Tip 1: Mindset Matters

Maintaining a positive, optimistic mindset is crucial, especially when facing insurmountable challenges. The power of positive thinking can significantly impact your ability to achieve goals and overcome obstacles. Everything began to shift for me when I decided I WAS going to get better. Despite being told that my condition was incurable, I chose to believe in my ability to heal and succeed. This unwavering optimism was instrumental in my recovery. Here's how you can cultivate a positive mindset:

- **Practice Gratitude**: Did you know that it is impossible to be grateful and sad or angry at the same time? It's true! Harness the power of gratitude to banish the nagging self-doubts that inevitably creep up. Start each day by listing things you are grateful for. When formulating your list, take the time to allow your body to be filled with gratitude. Just making a checklist of things you are grateful for isn't going to help; you need to deeply feel the emotion of gratitude associated with what you list. This exercise shifts your focus from what you believe is lacking to what's abundant, creating a positive outlook.

- **Visualize Success**: Spend time each day visualizing your inevitable success. Picture yourself achieving your goals and experiencing the positive outcomes. Try to really FEEL in your body that you have achieved your goal. All of the positive thinking in the world will not help you if you don't believe it in your core. While on my mission to restore my health, I would visualize myself running on a beach. I felt the wind in my face and the sand under my feet, could taste the salt splashing up from the water. Incorporating as many of the five senses as possible will make this exercise even more effective.

- **Mantras**: Create your own personal mantra to reprogram your subconscious mind. Statements like "I am capable of achieving great things" or "I am resilient and strong" can build confidence and resilience. Create something deeply personal so that it resonates for you.

- **Mindfulness and Meditation**: Stress is one of the biggest roadblocks to success and confidence. Practice simple mindfulness exercises to stay present and reduce stress, such as a few minutes of quiet block-breathing. These practices help you maintain a calm, positive state of mind, even in challenging situations.

Tip 2: Practice Self-Compassion

In pursuing health, wellness, and success, it's easy to be hard on yourself when things don't go as planned or move as quickly as you had hoped. Embracing self-compassion is a crucial element in building resilience and maintaining confidence. Recognize that you are human and that setbacks and mistakes are a natural part of any journey. Instead of seeing setbacks as failures, see them as valuable lessons that bring you closer to your goals. Here are a few ways to practice self-compassion:

- **Curiosity, Not Judgment**: When you suffer a setback or make a mistake, don't be so quick to mentally pummel yourself for the failure. I used to be famous for this behavior, believing that if I was ultra-hard on myself, I would excel. I was dead wrong; beating yourself up only creates more negativity. Instead, step back and think, "Isn't that curious; why did that happen?" Taking this break from the constant self-judgment will allow you to more deeply reflect on what drives your actions. In these moments of powerful self-reflection, you find the pearls of wisdom and real growth.

- **Be Kind to Yourself**: Think about how you would talk to a friend facing the same setbacks. Would you berate them and tell them that they were a disappointing failure? Of course not! Treat yourself with the same kindness and understanding you would offer that close friend. When you encounter inevitable challenges, remind yourself that it's okay to make mistakes and that these experiences are opportunities to learn and grow.

- **Acknowledge Your Efforts**: We often chase our goals so doggedly that we forget to celebrate the many small victories along the way. Instead of celebrating completing the marathon's first mile, we dwell on the remaining 25 miles. Give yourself a pat on the back for even small steps. These small celebrations acknowledge the effort you have put in and help to reinforce your confidence.

- **Challenge Negative Self-Talk**: ANTs are Automatic Negative Thoughts, made famous by Dr. Daniel Amen. He outlines a simple process to squash the negative thoughts that creep into our brains, crushing our confidence and self-esteem. Here are the steps to squash the ANTs.

As soon as you identify that you are triggered by negative thoughts, stop and ask yourself each of the following questions in this order:

- Is it true? (Is the negative thought actually true?)
- Can I absolutely know that it is true?
- How do I react when I think that thought?
- How would I feel if the opposite were true?

You will find as you run through the four questions that many of the negative thoughts that trigger you are actually just stories that you are telling yourself. Do not waste your energy on imaginary tales of misfortune. Throw your hat in the ring of life!

The more you deliberately practice squashing the ANTs, the more it will integrate seamlessly into your thought process.

Embracing self-compassion enhances emotional well-being and strengthens resilience, allowing you to bounce back from setbacks with greater ease. By being gentle with yourself, you create a supportive internal environment that fosters growth and confidence.

Incorporating self-compassion into your journey will help you maintain a balanced perspective, ensuring that you stay motivated and optimistic as you strive for personal and professional triumph. Remember, the path to success is not about perfection but about progress and self-love.

Tip 3: Borrow Bravery

Our brains are wired for survival, a fact that can sometimes work against us as we aspire to grow and change. The primitive part of our brain, often referred to as the "reptilian brain" or "lizard brain," is designed to keep us safe by avoiding risks and seeking familiarity. This instinctual drive served our ancestors well, helping them survive in a world full of physical dangers. However, in today's world, this same instinct can hold us back from pursuing new opportunities and achieving our full potential.

The primitive brain operates on the principle that it's better to stay in known misery, which is survivable, than to venture out into the unknown, which could be dangerous. This fear of the unknown can manifest as self-doubt, self-sabotage, procrastination, and an overwhelming urge to stick with the status quo, even when it's not serving us well.

When these fears kick in and hold you back, it can be incredibly empowering to "borrow" confidence from a trusted mentor. A mentor's belief in you can be a strong catalyst, helping you overcome self-doubt and take bold steps toward your goals. Surrounding yourself with mentors and positive influences can significantly boost your confidence. You can gain valuable insights and encouragement by seeking out and learning from those who have walked a similar path.

Two of my natural wellness mentors, Dr. Stephen Cabral and Dr. Ritamarie Loscalzo, played pivotal roles in my transformation from corporate leader to Integrative Health Practitioner. Their experiences, wisdom, and unwavering support provided me with the knowledge and inspiration needed to launch my own practice, even when I doubted myself. My marketing mentor, Molly Mahoney, gifted me the courage to really get out there and sell. Here's how you can apply this in your own life:

- **Identify Role Models**: Look for individuals who exemplify the courage and confidence you aspire to. This could be through their achievements in health, business, or personal growth.

- **Learn from Their Stories**: Read biographies, watch interviews, or attend talks by these role models. Let their journeys motivate you and provide you with practical tips and strategies.

- **Engage with a Mentor**: If possible, find a mentor who can provide you personalized guidance and support. Their experience can help you navigate challenges and keep you motivated.

- **Join Supportive Communities**: Engage in communities or groups that share your goals and values. Being part of a supportive network can provide encouragement, accountability, and shared wisdom.

Stepping Into a New Role

Making the transition from a safe and comfortable corporate career to launching a private practice as an Integrative Health Practitioner was not easy. Honestly, it was terrifying, but I was committed to my new path. I had to step out of my comfort zone and embrace a new identity. I had been very confident in my role in corporate leadership, and I was about to step out alone into a world where I was a newbie. Here are a few things I did to make this transition successfully:

Proper Mindset: I established a clear vision for my practice, focusing on helping hard-driving entrepreneurs achieve holistic health and increased success. More importantly, I believed to my core that I could help these women. This vision kept me motivated and guided my actions even when fears kicked in.

Practice Self-Compassion: I worked hard to train my ridiculously self-critical brain to look at myself with curiosity instead of harsh judgment. The time I took to step back and examine why I had behaved in specific ways illuminated many opportunities for growth, and I am much stronger for it.

Borrow Bravery: I surrounded myself with supportive individuals, including trusted mentors, family, and friends. Their encouragement and guidance were invaluable as I navigated this new path.

Conclusion

My journey from corporate leader to health and success coach has been marked by growth, resilience, and an unwavering commitment to empowering others. It has taught me the true meaning of courage and confidence. These qualities have transformed my life and enabled me to help countless women reclaim their health and live vibrant, fulfilling lives.

If you find yourself feeling overwhelmed, exhausted, or stuck, know that there is hope. You have the power within you to transform your life. Fine tune your mindset, embrace self-compassion, and borrow confidence when necessary. Your journey to a healthier, more successful life starts with a single courageous step.

Tracy Weskamp

Tracy Weskamp stands at the crossroads of integrative health and high-performance coaching, offering a revolutionary approach to wellness that empowers women to reclaim control over their health and lives. Her journey began with a successful corporate career, where she excelled in global leadership roles, marked by strategic innovation and team empowerment. This corporate foundation laid the groundwork for her transition to health and wellness.

Driven by a passion for helping others, especially women facing fatigue, brain fog, and weight challenges, Tracy immersed herself in holistic health studies, combining business acumen with knowledge in nutrition, genetics, and stress management. This blend culminated in the creation of the Body Mind Reboot Program, showcasing her commitment to holistic health and personal transformation.

Tracy's unique 5-Pillar Pathway to Peak Performance is more than just a program; it's a lifeline for women seeking to revive their youthful energy, focus, and confidence. She helps clients connect the dots between their symptoms and lifestyle, charting personalized paths forward that favor natural, sustainable solutions over pharmaceuticals.

As a sought-after speaker and coach, Tracy's impact extends beyond individual clients. Her workshops and speaking engagements inspire change, spark motivation, and impart practical wisdom. Tracy embodies the transformative power of integrative wellness, guiding women to awaken their inherent strength and step boldly into a brighter, healthier future.

Connect with Tracy at https://www.firemeuptracy.com.

CHAPTER 19

Experiential Impact: From Caves to Confidence

Wendy Barr

I'd like to dedicate this chapter to my amazing husband, whose unwavering support and inspiration push me to live life to the fullest. Your love and admiration fuel my creativity, boost my confidence, and drive my success. Thank you for being my rock and my biggest cheerleader.

This is a story about confidence—having faith in yourself and those around you. It's about not giving up and rejecting the notion that you're incapable or incomplete. Recently, I went on a beautiful vacation with my husband to Belize. The experience was magnificent: the sun shining, birds tweeting, and soft ocean waves lapping at the sand. The people were kind, generous, and easy-going. Their slogan is "go slow," but as an American, I didn't quite understand what that meant. I wake up every morning and jump on the treadmill of life, go-go-going until it's time to sleep, tossing and turning fitfully, only to wake up and start the cycle again. I was looking forward to relaxing on vacation.

Our plan was to spend a couple of nights in the jungle in San Ignacio, a few nights at the beach on Caye Caulker, and our last night in Belize City. I know what you're thinking—how can you relax with all that moving around? I agree, we didn't really think about that. My husband started researching excursions and found the ATM caves (Actun Tunichil Muknal). Located in the Mountain Tapir Reserve near the Guatemalan border, the ATM cave tour is rated as a soft to medium adventure. No problem, right? Online reviews described it as life-changing, the best tour they'd ever taken. Though it involved wading across rivers, hiking, swimming inside caves, and a bit of climbing, I thought I could handle it.

I was a bit alarmed when we read some of the reviews. One woman mentioned the tour was challenging and she was glad there were no older people with them. I told my husband, "Honey, I AM 'older people'! I'm not sure I can keep up." And the truth is that I've noticed my confidence waning as I grow older. "Age is just a number," he said and assured me that I could do this. After all, I'm physically fit, I walk my dog up and down hills every day, and I don't have any health issues. So, age be damned, I decided to unearth my sense of adventure, and we booked the excursion.

We arrived in Belize in the late afternoon and immediately drove an hour and a half inland to San Ignacio where we were staying. Our little jungle cabin was adorable! It had everything you would need: a screened-in patio, a kitchenette, a bathroom with actual plumbing, the perfect setting. But the tour was the next morning, leaving little time to sleep in or acclimate. I felt a bit annoyed, I wanted to relax, take it all in. I needed time to unwind and psych myself up for this adventure. But we were up at the crack of dawn, suited up in our gear, and waiting for the shuttle. The shuttle arrived and off we went, picking up a girl in her 30s traveling alone and a couple brimming with muscles and vigor. I felt older by the minute.

It was a long ride to the caves, and upon arrival, we were told no cameras or phones were allowed. We wore our swimsuits, water-resistant shorts, our specially purchased shoes and we were ready to go! We were also instructed to bring socks to wear inside the caves. Ummm, ok… Given helmets with headlamps, I started to panic but kept it to myself. I couldn't back out now and I didn't want anyone to know that I was apprehensive. We hiked through the forest for about 45 minutes on flat terrain with beautiful sights and sounds—leaf-cutter ants, howler monkeys, huge termite nests, squirrels, lizards, scorpions and fascinating vegetation.

The jungle was alive with a symphony of sounds, a vibrant chorus of life. There were plants I had never seen before, their leaves huge and glossy, their flowers bursting with colors so vivid they seemed unreal. The air was thick with the scent of earth and foliage, grounding me in the reality of this incredible place. I felt a mix of excitement and anxiety, knowing that our adventure was just beginning.

We arrived at the first water crossing and plunged into the shockingly cool, waist-deep river and waded across. Gasping along with the others, I felt in sync with the group. There were two more such crossings before we made it to the cave opening, fondly referred to as the "Cave of the Stone Sepulchre." Finally arriving at the cave entrance, we were greeted by a bright aqua pool of water surrounded by boulders and lush greenery. That's when we realized that our headlamps were the only source of light inside the cave. I was thrilled; I made it to the cave, I could relax now. Little did we know, the swimming, wading and hiking were far from over. Our final destination was still more than a mile into the cave, requiring us to navigate waters that varied from ankle-deep to well over our heads.

We hiked on slippery, sharp rocks, and as the terrain got rougher, it became harder to follow our guide's footsteps in the pitch black.

Immersed in darkness, the rocks scraped at my knees, my elbows bumped into rocks, and my heart pounded; I kept pushing forward. I began to question myself: "What did I get myself into?" There was a fright-night movie playing in my head. I thought about that woman who didn't want old people slowing her down and kept apologizing to my group. They were kind, reassuring me I was doing great.

The guide, recognizing my struggle, held my hand as we navigated the steep, slippery inclines. I distinctly remember being amazed that this dangerous adventure was even allowed. Liability much? I pushed forward. Memories of climbing ropes in gym class, getting to the top and panicking, frozen, refusing to move, unable to climb back down, as the other kids in class laughed and ridiculed me. And the time my girlfriend and I tried to sneak into a concert by climbing a very tall fence flashed in my mind. It wasn't the climb up that scared me, it was the paralyzing fear of climbing back down. She tried to coax me down, but I refused. Other kids that were climbing the fence tried to help me, "Put your right foot, then your left foot. It'll be okay." But it wasn't okay. I couldn't get down. I sat there panicking. I was embarrassed, mortified, and felt completely defeated.

So, there I was in the ATM caves, entering "The Cathedral" with bats flying overhead, feeling that same fear and lack of confidence. I had no choice but to keep going as there were other tour groups behind us and our guide kept us moving swiftly. So over the next few hours, we climbed higher: scaling rocks, climbing ladders, balancing on slippery underwater boulders and squeezing our necks through narrow rock passages which we dubbed the "guillotine rocks."

We continued our journey deeper into the darkness, marveling at the crystalline stalagmites and stalactites jutting from the cavern floor and ceiling, sparkling like diamonds when illuminated by our headlamps. It was incredible to think that these towering formations had been growing since the beginning of time, taking a thousand years to add just a few inches. The beauty of these natural formations was a stark contrast to the dark, eerie environment of the cave.

Eventually we reached a large chamber, the final destination of our journey. In the center lay the "Crystal Maiden"; her bones glistening with calcite deposits. It was a poignant sight, a reminder of the cave's role in ancient Mayan rituals. We stood in silence, each of us lost in our thoughts. I felt a profound connection to the past, a sense of awe at the resilience and spirituality of the Mayan people. This place, so remote and challenging to access, held such powerful stories.

When we entered the resting place of the Crystal Maiden, we removed our shoes and walked in socks to protect the artifacts. Seeing the damage caused by careless tourists made me appreciate the precaution. The sparkling skeleton of a likely sacrificial victim from 700-900 AD was chilling yet absolutely amazing! Nature's ability to create something breathtakingly beautiful over centuries reminded me that personal growth and building confidence is a gradual process.

As we stood there, our guide shared more about the significance of the Crystal Maiden. She was believed to have been sacrificed as part of a ritual to appease the gods, her life given in hopes of bringing prosperity to her community. You could see that the ribs around her heart were removed during the sacrifice. The calcification of her bones over centuries had given her a shimmering, almost ethereal appearance, adding to the sense of mystique surrounding her. It was a sobering reminder of the lengths to which people would go in the name of faith and survival.

The artifacts were incredible; ancient life coming alive before our eyes. Even in the dim light, the remnants of Mayan civilization were clearly and surprisingly intact. We saw urns, ceramics, stoneware, bones and skulls. Our guide told us that these artifacts had been used by shamans during rituals before conducting human sacrifices. The techniques they used were both creative and ruthless. From what I've read, the bones of over a dozen sacrificed men, women, and children have been found, and there was no question more were buried beneath the very ground on which we stood.

I was hoping that after all we went through to get to this point, we would just pop out of a back cave exit and land right back on the path through the jungle. That was not the case. We had to leave the same way we came in; climbing down the very rocks and boulders we scaled to get into this underground labyrinth. My stomach tightened, my heart pounded, but what choice did I have? With the help of our guide and my sweet, patient husband, I made my way back down, one step at a time. Sometimes sliding down rocks on my butt, crying a little on the inside, and holding the guide's hand so tight I thought I would break it, I kept going.

Despite the challenges, there were moments of beauty and wonder that made the journey worthwhile. The sight of the ancient pottery, the glittering crystals on the cave walls, and the knowledge that we were exploring a place of such historical significance kept me going. It was an adventure unlike any other, a true test of my physical and mental strength.

By the time we emerged from the cave, I was exhausted but elated. I had faced my fears, pushed my limits, and come out the other side with a newfound sense of confidence. The experience had shown me that I was capable of more than I had ever imagined, that age and self-doubt were no match for determination and courage. I felt a deep sense of accomplishment and gained the knowledge that I had done something truly extraordinary. Exhilaration washed over me. I had broken through so many fears and my confidence skyrocketed.

The adventure, however, was not over. When we arrived in Caye Caulker to our beautiful hotel room on the top floor that overlooked the deep turquoise ocean, we noticed there were bikes near the hotel lobby. Now, I don't know when I made the decision in my head that I was too old and frail to ride a bike, but the vision of my bike back home in the garage that I hadn't ridden for more than 10 years came vividly to mind. My husband voiced his apprehension for the same reason. Maybe that ship had sailed.

Before our trip, I remember someone telling me that golf carts were readily available and that we should rent one upon our arrival. So that was the plan. Based on the heat and humidity, my husband and I quickly realized that walking around the town was unrealistic. Not to mention, both of us were pretty sore from our cave excursion. But we looked at each other, climbed on the bikes and set off, wobbly and unsure of ourselves. I had forgotten how fun it was to ride a bike! These little beach cruisers took us all around the little island. Wind in our hair, wheels kicking up sand, we had a blast with our bikes and broke through yet another fear! My husband and I had a lot of fun together. We spent our days lounging on the beach, exploring the local culture, and savoring the delicious cuisine.

As we boarded the plane to head back home, I couldn't help but feel a sense of gratitude: grateful for the opportunity to explore such a remarkable place, for the support of my husband and the kindness of our fellow travelers, and for the inner strength that had carried me through. This trip had been an unexpected exploration of the fears I had unknowingly been harboring and that had kept me from reaching new heights.

Three Life-Changing Lessons from My (Wild & Wonderful) Adventure:

1. **Age is Just a Number:** Throughout my cave adventure, I learned that age doesn't define my capabilities. Despite my initial doubts and the fear of being "too old" to keep up, I realized that my physical fitness and determination were more than enough to conquer the challenges. This experience taught me that I shouldn't let age dictate what I can or cannot do. Confidence, resilience, and a willingness to push my limits

are far more important than the skewed societal perception of aging.

2. **Facing Fears Head-On:** My journey through the ATM caves and the subsequent bike ride around Caye Caulker were profound reminders that facing fears head-on is essential for personal growth. The movie playing in my head, memories of past embarrassments, and the paralyzing fear I felt all tried to hold me back. Yet, by confronting these fears and pushing through them, I discovered a newfound strength and confidence within myself. This experience underscored the importance of tackling fears directly, as the rewards on the other side are immense and transformative.

3. **Rediscovering Joy in Simple Pleasures:** Riding a bike after so many years brought back a simple, pure joy that I had almost forgotten. This trip reminded me of the importance of reconnecting with activities that bring me joy, no matter how small or seemingly insignificant. Sometimes, the simplest pleasures can reignite a sense of freedom and happiness, reminding us to take a break from our busy lives and enjoy the little things.

I've also learned to embrace imperfection and that it's perfectly okay to show vulnerability. This experience reinforced that true confidence comes from accepting and overcoming our flaws, not from pretending they don't exist. This adventure was a significant chapter in my ongoing journey of self-discovery. It reminded me that learning and growth are continuous processes. And that the journey of discovering inner strength and confidence doesn't have a final destination; it's an ever-evolving path that enriches life in countless ways. And guess what, it's okay to lean on others for help, because their belief in your abilities can catapult your own confidence. The kindness and support from my husband and fellow travelers reminded me that I don't have to face life's challenges alone; a supportive network can make all the difference.

Overall, these experiences showed me that I can face any challenge that comes my way. After this trip, I'm ready to tackle ziplining, windsurfing, you name it and I'll try it. Well, maybe...baby steps.

Now that I'm back in the routine of daily life, I carry the lessons of that adventure deep within me. I am more confident, more willing to take on new challenges, and more aware of the strength that lies within me. Belize was more than just a vacation—it was a journey of self-discovery, one that I will cherish for the rest of my life.

This transformative experience has deepened my commitment to empowering small business owners to make a greater impact on the world. With over 20 years of experience in branding and marketing, and a Master's degree in branding and design, I have dedicated myself to helping small businesses and entrepreneurs leverage the power of AI in their branding and marketing efforts. My programs, offerings, courses, and curated communities provide entrepreneurs with actionable insights they can apply immediately to connect emotionally with their ideal clients, increase visibility, ensure profitability, and drive significant change.

I am particularly committed to empowering women in business by connecting them to a supportive network of women business owners and female professionals. My mission is to catapult experts, entrepreneurs, and small businesses to success by building trust and credibility through authentic human connections. By empowering entrepreneurs globally, I strive to make a lasting impact, helping them realize their potential and make a meaningful difference in the world.

Connect with me on all the socials! @iamwendybarr

See what I'm up to at www.intelligentbrands.ai.

PROFIT BOOSTER AI BRAND ASSESSMENT:

Clarity makes all the difference! Schedule your complimentary, laser-focused 1:1 Brand Consult Call to identify your unique distinctions, boost your visibility and profitability, and outline your next steps. Your impact matters—let's make it happen!

https://members.intelligentbrands.ai/PBBA

10 Steps to Activate Your AI Brand CHEATSHEET:

If you are using ChatGPT and other AI tools to generate marketing and brand awareness content, you need to teach AI to speak in your BRAND VOICE. You only have one chance to make a great first impression and studies say that you have approximately seven seconds to grab their attention.

Let's get you started!

https://members.intelligentbrands.ai/aiActivate

Wendy Barr

Wendy Barr is a business visionary with over 20 years of experience in branding and marketing. She's passionate about helping small business owners harness the power of AI to create unique, authentic brands that align with their values and emotionally connect with their ideal clients. Her proprietary approach is key to building sustainable, profitable businesses and exponentially increase brand visibility.

With a Master's degree in branding and design, Wendy has extensive experience teaching college-level courses in branding and marketing. She has worked with world-renowned brands like MTV, Allure Magazine, Jive Records, and Rockefeller Center. Wendy's mission is to propel experts, entrepreneurs, and small businesses to success by building trust and credibility through genuine human connections. Her programs empower entrepreneurs globally, providing actionable insights they can immediately apply to their businesses.

Connect with Wendy at www.intelligentbrands.ai.

READER BONUS!

Dear Reader,

As a thank you for your support, the Authors of *Choose Confidence* would like to offer you a special reader bonus.

Go here to tap into the free gifts from the authors valued at more than $10,000: www.ChooseConfidence.com.

READER BONUS!

Made in the USA
Columbia, SC
14 August 2024

40469399R00137